CHEF TELL'S QUICK CUISINE

Gourmet Cooking
Simple, Fast, Delicious

by

TELL ERHARDT

with Rosalyn T. Badalamenti

Photographs by Stanley E. Madey

WARNER BOOKS

A Warner Communications Company

Copyright © 1982 by International Cuisine, Inc.

Warner Books, Inc., 75 Rockefeller Plaza, New York, N.Y. 10019.

A Warner Communications Company

Printed in the United States of America

First printing: May 1982

10 9 8 7 6 5 4 3 2 1

Book Design by *H. Roberts Design*
Jacket Design by *Gene Light*

Library of Congress Cataloging in Publication Data

Erhardt, Tell.
　Chef Tell's quick cuisine.

　1. Cookery.　I. Badalamenti, Rosalyn T.
II. Title.　III. Title: Quick cuisine.
TX652.E6　　　641.5　　　81-19870
ISBN 0-446-51240-0　　　　AACR2

To
My mother, Giesela, and to my father, Max,

and to
all those people in the United States
who had enough faith in me
to help me get started here.

—T.E.

To
My mother, Lucy Badalamenti,
who taught me about the
important things of life.

—R.T.B.

Contents

Preface

I think I became a chef because I was always hungry when I was growing up. You see, I grew up in post-World War II Germany, and there just wasn't that much food around in those days. My mother had to create our meals out of CARE packages and magic, and I would watch her as she cooked, sampling, of course, but also learning.

When I became a Master Chef, I still remembered my mother's way with food, and I realized that all those techniques I had learned during my training could be simplified so that anyone could feel competent in the kitchen.

And that's why I decided to write this book. For years now, I have been sharing my ideas with my audiences on TV and in public appearances. But I felt that there should be a permanent record, one that you, my friends, could hold in your hands and get comfort from in the kitchen.

The recipes in this book are very simple, very easy—nothing to be afraid of. They will help you prepare food that will make your taste buds say, "I want some." I have demonstrated many of these recipes on TV and have also used them in my cooking school.

There are a few things you should remember when you begin to plan a meal. Food is very sensuous. So, when you cook, you have to consider eye appeal, smell, taste, texture, and digestion.

Smell is very important. That is why the nose is above the mouth. When something smells good, your taste buds are activated and you get the full flavor of the food.

Texture is also very important, though it is often ignored. You must put the right foods together so that your digestive juices will work properly. If you don't, you may feel rotten for days after eating a meal. That's why I have made suggestions for serving accompaniments in some of the recipes.

There are two things you can do before you start cooking that will make it easier for you to prepare any dish. First, read the recipe through a few times to make sure you know what you have to do. Then, assemble your ingredients all in one place so that you don't have to hunt around for anything you need while you are making the dish. Incidentally, if you don't have a spice or a vegetable called for in a recipe, make a substitution, or leave it out. Recipes are only guidelines, not commandments, so you can change them, within reason, if necessary.

Just remember, I have prepared all these dishes the long and complicated way, and I have already made the mistakes. If you follow my directions, you will enjoy yourself in the kitchen and produce delicious food, too.

Good cooking! Good eating!

1
The Basic Skills

Do you know the difference between mincing and chopping? Do you want to know the easy way to peel a tomato? Both are really very simple. Let me show you how to do those things, and how to cut up a chicken, carve a turkey, and make quenelles. It's easy when you know how, and all you have to do is practice to gain confidence.

TECHNIQUE FOR CHOPPING

1. Peel the onion, making sure you do not cut off the root end. Slice the onion in half lengthwise.

2. Lay one onion half, cut side down, on the chopping board. Cut through the onion at ¼-inch intervals, about two thirds of the way down to the root end.

3. Slice the onion half once or twice horizontally, being careful not to cut through the root end or your fingers.

4. Chop the onion from top to bottom at about ⅛-inch intervals.

2

TECHNIQUE FOR MINCING

1. Peel the onion, making sure you do not cut off the root end. Slice the onion in half lengthwise.

2. Lay one onion half, cut side down, on the chopping board. Cut through the onion at ⅛-inch intervals, about two thirds of the way down to the root end.

3. Slice the onion half once or twice horizontally, being careful not to cut through the root end or your fingers.

4. Using your index finger as a guide, slice the onion as thinly as possible from top to bottom.

3

TECHNIQUE FOR DICING

1. Slice the vegetables into ¼-inch-thick slices.

2. Stack two or three slices on top of each other and cut them into ¼-inch sticks.

3. Cut the sticks into ¼-inch lengths.

TECHNIQUE FOR JULIENNING

1. Cut the peeled carrot and the trimmed celery into 3-inch lengths. Slice each length of carrot into ⅛-inch-thick slices.

2. Stack two or three carrot slices on top of each other and cut into ⅛-inch sticks. Cut the celery lengths into ⅛-inch sticks.

TECHNIQUE FOR PEELING TOMATOES

1. Cut the core out of each tomato with a paring knife.

2. Turn the tomatoes over and cut a shallow cross on the side opposite the stem end.

3. Bring a small pot of water to boil, add the tomatoes, and turn off the heat. Leave the tomatoes in the water for 2 minutes. You will see that the skin around the cross will start to come loose.

4. Remove the tomatoes from the hot water and put them in a container of cold water. Peel off the skin, starting at the cross.

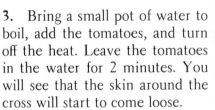

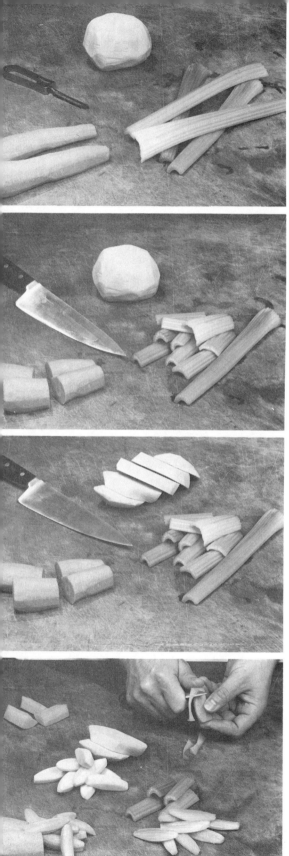

TECHNIQUE FOR MAKING TURNED VEGETABLES

1. Scrape the celery and carrots slightly and peel the turnip.

2. Cut the carrots and celery into 2½-inch lengths.

3. Cut the turnip into ¾-inch-thick slices.

4. Trim each of the vegetable pieces into an oval shape.

7

TECHNIQUE
FOR CUTTING UP
A CHICKEN

1. Put the chicken on a cutting board, sitting up, with the backbone facing you. With a very sharp knife, cut through the back of the chicken down one side of the backbone.

2. Flatten the chicken, pressing the backbone to the cutting board and cut along the other side of the backbone to remove it completely.

3. Put the chicken, breast side down, on the board and use your fingers to break out the center breastbone. Remove it and any cartilage attached to it. Cut the chicken in half through the center of the breast.

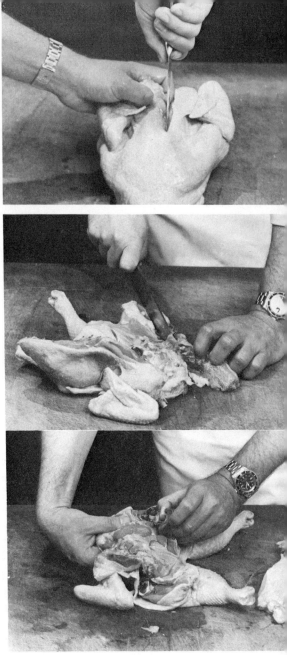

4. Turn the chicken halves skin side up. Cut through each half to separate the breasts from the legs.

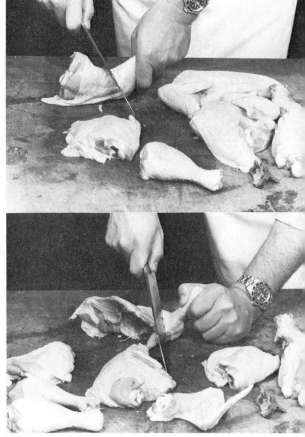

5. Take each leg in your left hand and use your right hand to bend the thigh portion back until you can see where the joint is. Cut through at this point to sever the drumstick from the thigh.

6. Put the chicken breast, with wings attached, on its side. Bend the wing back until you can see where the joint is. Cut through at this point to sever the wing from the breast.

TECHNIQUE FOR SKINNING AND BONING CHICKEN THIGHS AND DRUMSTICKS

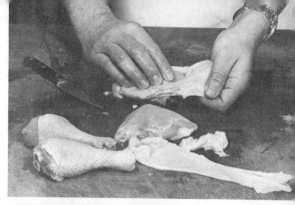

1. Pull the skin off the thigh with your fingers.

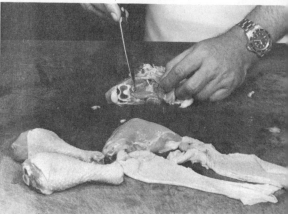

2. Turn the thigh over and insert the tip of your knife very close to one side of the thigh bone. Work the knife up and down the length of the bone until the meat is free.

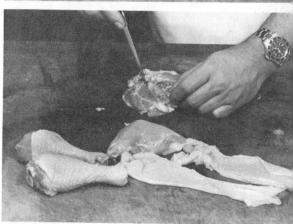

3. Insert the knife under the top flap of meat over the bone and work it up and down the length of the bone until the meat is free. The bone should be almost completely exposed now.

4. Spread the meat out so that you can insert your knife under the bone. Work the knife up and down to free the bone completely.

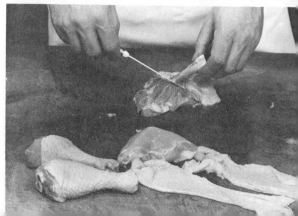

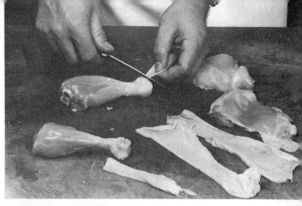

5. Pull the skin of the drumstick down to the bottom and cut it off.

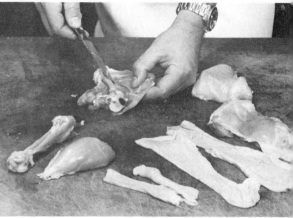

6. Lay the drumstick on the cutting board and cut through the meat straight to the bone.

7. Cut around the bottom of the drumstick to free the meat.

8. Work the tip of your knife up, down, and around the bone until the meat is free.

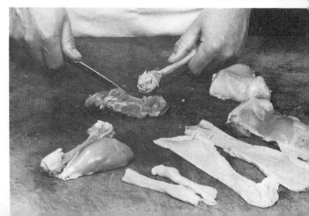

TECHNIQUE FOR SKINNING AND BONING CHICKEN BREASTS

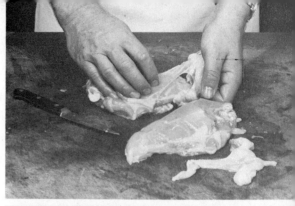

1. Pull the skin off the breast with your fingers.

2. Turn the breast over and place it so that the ribs of the chicken are facing you.

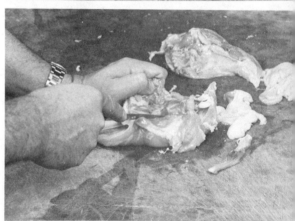

3. Insert the tip of your knife between the flesh and the bone, as close to the bone as possible. Work the tip of the knife back and forth until you have freed about ½ inch of the meat all along the bone.

4. Turn the breast over and use the blade of the knife to free the meat completely from the bone.

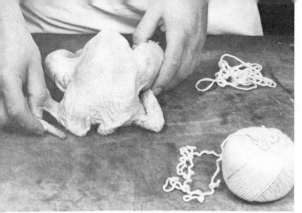

TECHNIQUE FOR TRUSSING A CHICKEN

1. Cut off about 4 feet of heavy kitchen string. Turn the wing tips back underneath the chicken.

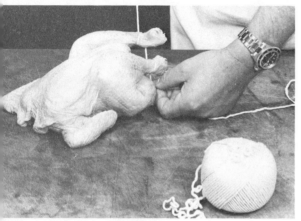

2. Leave about 6 inches of string free and loop the string around the end of one drumstick. Carry it outside and loop it around the other drumstick.

3. Tuck the loose neck skin under the chicken. Bring the string up and around, circling the chicken, between the wings and around the neck.

4. Bring up the free end of the string and, pulling it tight, tie the two ends together on the side of the thigh.

13

TECHNIQUE FOR POUNDING AND BREADING CUTLETS

1. Lay the cutlets flat on the cutting board and pound them lightly on both sides with a flat mallet. This will tenderize the meat by breaking down some of its cell structure; it will also help to make an even layer of meat.

2. In a flat soup plate, beat 2 eggs until they are well combined.

3. Put a good amount of all-purpose flour on a large square of wax paper. Put an equal amount of bread crumbs on another large square of wax paper.

4. Dredge each cutlet in the flour. Then dip it into the beaten egg and then into the bread crumbs. Use the excess wax paper to toss the bread crumbs on top of the cutlet.

5. Press the bread crumbs onto the cutlet with the palm of your hand. Turn the cutlet over, toss the bread crumbs on top again, and press them in again with your palm.

6. As the cutlets are breaded, put them on a flat dish, making sure they do not touch. Separate the layers of cutlets with wax paper. Refrigerate for 10 minutes before sautéeing.

See page 16 for technique for skinning and boning chicken breasts.

TECHNIQUE FOR TYING A ROAST

1. Starting at one end of the meat, loop heavy kitchen string around the meat and tie a knot, leaving a few inches of string free.

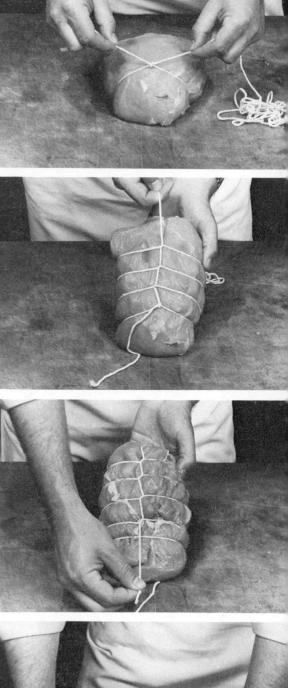

2. Then, at approximately 2-inch intervals, bring the string under and around the meat, holding the string on top of the meat straight with your left hand. Form a knot by looping the long piece of string over, around, and through this straight piece of string. Pull the knot tight while holding the string straight. Repeat this procedure until you reach the other end of the meat.

3. Turn the meat over and pull the string under and around each circular loop so that it forms a straight line down the center of the meat.

4. When you reach the end of the meat, tie a knot, using the end of the string you left free previously.

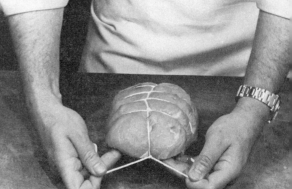

TECHNIQUE FOR FORMING QUENELLES

1. Moisten your hand with cold water and spread a layer of the farce on your palm.

2. Use a teaspoon to form the quenelles by scraping up about a teaspoon of the mixture to form little cylinders.

3. With the end of your finger, push each cylinder off the teaspoon into the simmering stock.

TECHNIQUE FOR CARVING A TURKEY

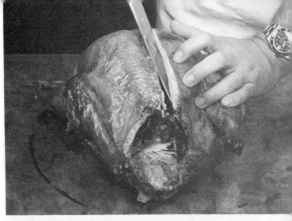

1. With your carving knife, cut down on one side of the breast-bone. Then continue cutting up to the wishbone and down to the wing.

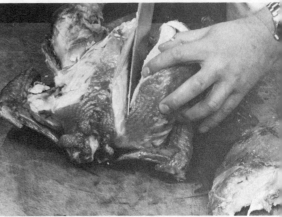

2. Remove the whole breast in one piece. Remove the breast meat from the other side in the same manner.

3. Slice the breast meat at an angle and arrange the slices on a platter.

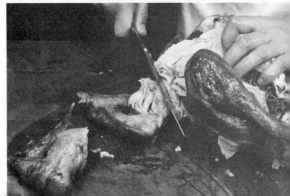

4. Cut off the wings and add them to the platter.

5. Pull the legs away from the carcass and cut through the joints to remove the whole leg.

6. Cut through the joint to separate the thighs from the drumsticks. Add the drumsticks to the platter.

7. Slice some of the meat from the thighs and add it to the platter.

8. The carved turkey is ready to be served.

TECHNIQUE FOR CHOOSING COOKWARE

1. Choose cookware of heavy cast aluminum. A good basic set includes a 5-quart Dutch oven, 2-quart saucepan, 1-quart saucepan, 9-inch frying pan, deep-fat fryer, and an 11-inch frying pan. The silverstone lining is an added bonus.

2. A highly polished finish resists stains and lasts longer than enamel or regular aluminum. See how snugly the cover fits; that's important.

3. The nice round shape of this Dutch oven makes it easier to stir those long-cooking stews. The silverstone lining will let you use less oil or butter when cooking, and your food won't stick to the surface of the pot.

4. Even your smaller saucepans should have tight-fitting covers.

5.   The raised bottom of this 9-inch frying pan gives it good balance and even heat distribution.

6.   A wooden handle will not conduct heat, so you will not burn yourself, no matter how high a flame you use. The straight sides of this deep-fat fryer are high enough to prevent splattering.

7.   The thick aluminum bottom of this 11-inch frying pan will not warp, so that you will always have even heat distribution.

8.   The wide flaring sides of this 11-inch frying pan will make it easier to sauté like a professional chef.

2
Appetizers

German Onion Tart, Ham Cornets with Aspic, and
Poached Pears with Liver.

Sometimes you want to start off dinner with a little something
extra—just to make it more special. Here are some appetizer
dishes you can make easily, and they will turn any dinner into a
celebration.

Fried Camembert

6 SERVINGS

1 or 2 bunches of parsley sprigs
   Flour for dredging
2 eggs beaten with 1 tablespoon
   water

Bread crumbs
1 not-too-ripe wheel of
   Camembert
Vegetable oil

1. Wash the parsley sprigs and dry them well. Set them aside.

2. Pour enough flour to coat the cheese on a piece of wax paper. Put the eggs and water in a flat soup plate and beat them together. Put enough bread crumbs to coat the cheese on a piece of wax paper.

3. Cut the cheese into slices. Dip each slice first in the flour, to coat both sides. Then turn it in the egg, to coat both sides. Coat the slice completely with bread crumbs, pressing the crumbs on with the palm of your hand (see p. 15). Put the breaded cheese slices on a plate, making sure they do not touch. Separate the layers with wax paper. Chill for 10 minutes.

4. Pour about ½ inch oil into a frying pan and heat it. Carefully add the coated cheese slices. Cook for 1 or 2 minutes, or until they are golden brown on both sides. As the slices brown, drain them on paper towels.

5. Arrange the drained cheese slices in an overlapping circle on a serving platter.

6. Plunge the well-dried parsley into the hot oil and cook until crisp. This will take only 1 minute. Arrange the fried parsley in the center of the platter. Serve the dish immediately.

Stuffed Cucumbers

6 SERVINGS

3 large cucumbers
1 8-ounce package cream
 cheese, softened
3 tablespoons finely minced
 onion

½ teaspoon paprika
 Salt
 Freshly ground black pepper
1 cup finely chopped parsley
 Lettuce leaves

1. Trim the ends off the cucumbers, and cut the cucumbers into 1½-inch lengths. Peel the skin off one half of each segment. Remove the seeds from the center of the sections about two thirds of the way down, leaving the bottom intact. Turn the cucumber shells upside down to drain.

2. Whip the cream cheese until it is fluffy. Add the onion, paprika, and salt and pepper to taste. Form the mixture into enough small balls to fill the cucumber shells. Roll the balls in the chopped parsley and put one in each cucumber shell.

3. Line six small serving plates with lettuce leaves and distribute the stuffed cucumbers among them. Serve very cold.

Ham Cornets with Aspic

8 SERVINGS

16 slices boiled ham
 2 8-ounce packages cream
 cheese, softened
 2 tablespoons drained
 horseradish

 Heavy cream (optional)
 2 cups fat-free consommé or
 beef bouillon
 2 tablespoons unflavored
 gelatin

1. Cut each ham slice into two triangles. Roll each triangle into a cornet and secure with a toothpick.

2. Beat the cream cheese with a hand mixer until it is fluffy. Mix in the horseradish. Thin the mixture to piping consistency with the heavy cream, if necessary. Put the cream cheese mixture into a pastry bag with a star-shaped nozzle and pipe it into the cornets decoratively.

3. Arrange the cornets in a small circle on a serving plate. Place the next row of cornets facing in the opposite direction, alternating rows to form a dome-shaped mound. Chill.

4. Put the consommé in a small saucepan and add the gelatin. Let it soften for a few minutes. When the gelatin has softened, heat the mixture, stirring to dissolve the gelatin completely. Cool and chill until the aspic is the consistency of unbeaten egg whites. Brush the liquid aspic over the cornets and chill until set.

Stuffed Ham Rolls

6 SERVINGS

1 tablespoon unflavored gelatin	3 tablespoons drained
Juice of 1 lemon	horseradish
¼ cup water	12 slices boiled ham
1 cup heavy cream	

1. Soften the gelatin in the lemon juice and water. Heat, stirring, to dissolve the gelatin completely. Cool to lukewarm.

2. Whip the cream lightly (not until it is stiff, but until it just begins to hold soft peaks). Stir in the horseradish and cooled gelatin mixture.

3. Lay the ham slices on a flat surface so they are not overlapping. Spread the cream mixture evenly over the slices, smoothing it with a small spatula. Chill until the cream mixture thickens a little.

4. Roll the ham slices up and return them to the refrigerator until the cream sets. Serve two rolls per person.

Rolled Fish Mousse

6 SERVINGS

½ pound fluke or flounder fillets
3 egg whites
6 tablespoons butter or
    margarine
  Salt
  Freshly ground black pepper
1 cup spinach leaves, blanched
    and squeezed dry (optional)

⅔ cup heavy cream, lightly
    beaten
6 fillets of sole
½ cup dry white wine
1 tablespoon minced onion
¼ cup heavy cream, lightly
    beaten

1. Put the ½ pound fish fillets into the container of a blender or food processor and grind them thoroughly. With the motor on, add the egg whites one at a time, beating after each addition. Add the butter and blend again. Season with salt and pepper to taste and turn the mixture into a bowl. Cover and refrigerate until well chilled. If you want to add the spinach, remove only half the purée and process the spinach with the purée left in the machine. This will give you two types of mousse, which will make the dish very pretty.

2. When the mousse is well chilled, fold in the lightly beaten cream.

3. Cut the fillets in half so that you have twelve long strips. Place them flat with the skin side up. This way they will not fall apart when you cook them.

4. Spread a small amount of either the plain fish mousse or the spinach fish mousse over each fillet. Roll the fillets up tightly. Put the rolled fillets, seam side down, in a frying pan large enough to hold them comfortably. Pour the wine around the fillets and poach them over low heat for 25 minutes. Carefully remove the fish rolls to a platter and keep them warm.

5. Add the minced onion to the frying pan, raise the heat, and reduce the wine and fish juices by half. Add the lightly whipped cream and reduce by half again. Pour the sauce over the fish rolls and serve immediately.

Smoked Salmon Mousse

6 SERVINGS

6 tablespoons butter or margarine
3 tablespoons all-purpose flour
1¼ cups milk, heated
1 tablespoon unflavored gelatin
4 tablespoons water
1 3-ounce package cream cheese, softened
2 tablespoons grated Parmesan cheese
4 slices smoked salmon
3 egg yolks
Salt
Freshly ground black pepper
Pinch of cayenne pepper
3 egg whites
⅔ cup heavy cream

1. Melt 3 tablespoons of butter in a saucepan and add the flour all at once, stirring to make a smooth, creamy mixture. Gradually stir in the hot milk. Bring to a boil, lower the heat, and simmer for 4 to 5 minutes, stirring occasionally. Remove from the heat and let cool a bit.

2. Soften the gelatin in the water.

3. Pour the milk mixture into the container of a blender. Add the gelatin mixture and blend until smooth. Add the cream cheese, Parmesan cheese, and salmon. Blend until smooth. Add the egg yolks one at a time, continuing to blend after each addition. Scrape the purée into a large bowl and season it with salt and pepper to taste and cayenne. Let the purée cool a little.

4. Use the remaining 3 tablespoons of butter to butter a mold for the mousse. Put the buttered mold in the refrigerator to chill.

5. Whip the egg whites until they are stiff. Without cleaning the beaters, whip the cream until it holds stiff peaks. Fold the egg whites and whipped cream into the cooled purée. Pour the mousse into the prepared mold and chill until set. Unmold and garnish as desired.

Cold Chicken Liver Mousse

6 TO 8 SERVINGS

Butter or margarine
½ pound chicken livers,
    trimmed of all fat
½ clove garlic, peeled and
    crushed
¼ cup all-purpose flour
4 eggs

4 egg yolks
1½ cups milk
¼ cup heavy cream
Pinch of ground nutmeg
Salt
Freshly ground black pepper
Hot toast

1. Butter the inside of a 2-quart mold or soufflé dish. Line the bottom with a piece of parchment paper and butter the paper. Set the mold aside.

2. Put the chicken livers and garlic in the container of a blender or food processor. Purée until smooth. Sprinkle the flour on top and mix it into the puréed livers with a rubber spatula. Add the eggs one at a time, blending after each addition. Add the egg yolks, milk, and cream, also blending after each addition. Then add the nutmeg and salt and pepper to taste.

3. Pour the mousse into the prepared mold. It should be about three-quarters full.

4. Preheat the oven to 325 degrees.

5. Set the mold into a baking pan and pour in enough hot water to come halfway up the sides of the mold. Heat on top of the stove until the water is just simmering. Transfer to the oven and bake for 40 to 50 minutes, or until a skewer inserted in the center comes out clean. Remove the mold from the water bath and let it cool.

6. Unmold and serve with hot toast.

NOTE: For a mousse with a smoother texture, the mixture can be passed through a sieve before it is put into the mold.

Poached Pears with Liver

6 SERVINGS

3 ripe pears
2 cups plus 4 tablespoons water
¼ cup sugar
Juice of ½ lemon
4 tablespoons butter or
  margarine
1 pound chicken livers, trimmed
  of all fat

3 tablespoons port wine
3 tablespoons brandy
2 tablespoons unflavored gelatin
Salt
Freshly ground black pepper
½ cup heavy cream, whipped
Pitted black olives for garnish

1. Cut the pears in half and remove the cores.

2. Combine 2 cups of water, the sugar, and the lemon juice in a saucepan. Bring to a boil, add the pear halves, and poach until the pears are just barely tender. Remove the pears with a slotted spoon and let them drain.

3. Melt the butter in a small frying pan and add the livers. Sauté the livers for 1 or 2 minutes, until they are just cooked. Remove the livers to a bowl. Pour the port into the skillet and deglaze the pan. Add the port to the livers in the bowl. Add the brandy to the skillet and deglaze again. Add the brandy to the livers. Cool the livers and then purée them with the liquids.

4. Put the gelatin and the 4 tablespoons of water into a small saucepan. Let the gelatin soften and then heat gently, stirring until it completely dissolves. Add to the puréed liver and season with salt and pepper to taste. Fold in the whipped cream completely and chill for several hours.

5. Put the chilled liver mousse in a pastry bag with a star-shaped nozzle. Pipe the liver mousse onto the pear halves so that the pears look as if they are whole again. Decorate with slices of black olives. Serve chilled.

Vegetable Terrine

6 SERVINGS

½ pound dried white beans picked over
4 carrots, trimmed, scraped, and julienned
1 cup frozen peas
½ pound string beans, trimmed
1 box fresh brussels sprouts
6 slices trimmed white bread
5 tablespoons butter or margarine

1 small onion, peeled and minced
2 cloves garlic, peeled and minced
¼ pound mushrooms, chopped
2 eggs
1 egg yolk
2 tablespoons chopped parsley
Salt
Freshly ground black pepper

1. Soak the white beans overnight in water to cover by 1 inch. Drain the beans, add water to cover and salt to taste. Bring to a boil, cover, lower the heat, and cook until tender.

2. Cook the carrots, peas, string beans, and brussels sprouts separately in boiling salted water. Cook each vegetable until it is just barely tender. Drain each and refresh under cold running water and drain again. Slice the brussels sprouts in half.

3. Drain the cooked white beans and put them through a food mill to purée them. Set the purée aside.

4. Soak the bread in water to cover until it is soft. Squeeze dry and set aside.

5. Melt 2 tablespoons of butter in a small frying pan. Add the onion and garlic and sauté until soft. Add the mushrooms and cook until the mixture is dry.

6. Mix together the white bean purée, the mushrooms, bread, eggs, egg yolk, and parsley. Season with salt and pepper to taste.

7. Use the remaining butter to butter a terrine mold. (Use a mold with removable sides, if possible.)

8. Alternate layers of the bean mixture and the vegetables decoratively in the mold, beginning and ending with the bean mixture.

9. Preheat the oven to 350 degrees.

10. Cover the mold tightly with buttered foil, buttered side down. Bake the terrine for 60 to 75 minutes. Cool and then chill overnight in the refrigerator. Unmold and serve in slices with cornichons on the side.

Molded Liver Pâté

6 SERVINGS

2 pounds chicken or calves' liver
1 cup plus 2 tablespoons port or
    Madeira wine
1 cup butter or margarine
1 onion, peeled and chopped
Juice of 1 lemon
Pinch of dried thyme
Pinch of ground allspice

Salt
Freshly ground black pepper
⅔ cup heavy cream
2 cups fat-free consommé or
    beef bouillon
2 tablespoons unflavored gelatin
Pimiento cutouts for garnish

1. Marinate the livers in 1 cup port for 2 hours, turning occasionally. Drain the livers, but reserve the marinade.

2. Melt ½ cup butter in a frying pan. Add the onion and sauté until soft. Add the drained livers, lemon juice, thyme, allspice, and salt and pepper to taste. Sauté, tossing gently, until the livers are brown on the outside but still pink inside. Put the liver mixture in the container of a blender or food processor.

3. Deglaze the frying pan with the reserved marinade. Add it to the blender container.

4. Purée the liver mixture until it is smooth. Add the cream and the remaining butter and blend again. Correct the seasonings, if necessary.

5. Either line a mold with a damp piece of cheesecloth or butter it well. Pour the pâté into the mold, packing it down firmly. Chill overnight.

6. Combine the consommé and the gelatin in a small saucepan. When the gelatin is softened, heat, stirring, until it is completely dissolved. Let cool to room temperature. Stir in the remaining 2 tablespoons of port and chill the aspic until it is the consistency of unbeaten egg whites.

7. Unmold the pâté onto a serving plate. Decorate it with pimiento cutouts. Brush one or two layers of aspic over the decorated pâté, making sure to chill the first layer before adding the second.

Curried Beef in Pastry

6 SERVINGS

1½ cups all-purpose flour
  Salt
10 tablespoons butter or
    margarine
 4 tablespoons ice water
 2 tablespoons vegetable oil
 1 cup minced onion
 1 small clove garlic, peeled and
    minced

1½ teaspoons curry powder
 ¾ pound lean ground beef
    Freshly ground black pepper
    Pinch of sugar
 3 tablespoons ketchup
 ½ teaspoon cornstarch
 3 teaspoons water
 1 tablespoon bread crumbs
 1 egg, beaten

1. Put the flour into a bowl with 1 teaspoon of salt. Cut in the butter, using a pastry blender or two knives, until the mixture resembles coarse meal. Add only enough water to combine the mixture until it leaves the sides of the bowl and forms a ball. Work quickly and do not overwork the dough. Cover the bowl and refrigerate while you prepare the filling.

2. Heat the oil in a frying pan and add the onion and garlic. Sauté until soft. Add the curry powder, ground beef, and salt and pepper to taste. Cook, stirring, until the beef is browned. Add the sugar and ketchup and cook 2 minutes longer. Remove from the heat. Mix the cornstarch with the water and stir into the beef mixture. Add the bread crumbs and mix well. Chill completely.

3. Divide the dough in half. Roll out one portion and cut out twelve 2-inch rounds. Roll out the second portion and cut out twelve more 2-inch rounds.

4. Divide the beef mixture evenly among twelve rounds, piling it in the center of each round. Moisten the edges of each round with water. Press a second round of dough over the filling and seal the edges with your fingers.

5. Preheat the oven to 375 degrees.

6. Put the filled pastries on a buttered baking sheet. Brush each with some beaten egg. Bake for 35 minutes, or until brown.

Mushroom Strudel

12 SERVINGS

2 tablespoons butter or
  margarine
1 small onion, peeled and
  minced
1 pound mushrooms, minced
  Salt
  Freshly ground black pepper

1 8-ounce package cream
  cheese, softened
12 sheets filo leaves
½ cup melted butter or
  margarine
1 cup toasted bread crumbs

1. Melt 2 tablespoons of butter in a frying pan. Add the onion
and sauté for 5 minutes. Add the mushrooms and salt and pepper to
taste. Cook, stirring occasionally, until the mixture is dry. Let the mixture cool for a few minutes, then stir in the cream cheese.

2. Spread the filo leaves out, keeping those you are not working
with covered with a damp towel.

3. Place one filo leaf in front of you on a clean towel. Brush it
with melted butter and sprinkle with a thin layer of bread crumbs.
Repeat three more times to make a total of four layers. Do not butter
or bread-crumb the top layer. Spread one third of the filling down the
length of the filo, 2 inches in from the edge. Fold the 2-inch flap of filo
over the stuffing, fold in the sides, and roll up the rest of the dough,
using the towel as leverage to pull the roll tight. Put the completed
roll on a buttered baking sheet and brush the top of the roll with
melted butter. Repeat the entire process two more times with the
remaining filo leaves.

4. Preheat the oven to 400 degrees.

5. Bake the rolls for 25 to 30 minutes, or until brown and crisp.
Slice and serve warm.

NOTE: The rolls can be prepared to the end of Step 3 and kept in
the refrigerator for several hours or overnight. Just cover the rolls with
foil before you refrigerate them. Take them out of the refrigerator ½
hour before you plan to bake them and keep them covered until just
before you put them in the oven. Spread them with more melted butter before baking.

Spinach and Cheese Strudel

12 SERVINGS

1 10-ounce package frozen leaf
    spinach
2 tablespoons butter or
    margarine
1 onion, peeled and minced
1 15-ounce container ricotta
    cheese
2 eggs
½ cup grated Gruyère cheese

Pinch of ground nutmeg
Salt
Freshly ground black pepper
1 to 2 tablespoons all-purpose
    flour (optional)
12 sheets filo leaves
½ cup melted butter or
    margarine
1 cup toasted bread crumbs

1. Parboil the spinach in boiling salted water. Refresh under cold running water, drain, and squeeze dry. Chop fine and set aside.

2. Melt 2 tablespoons of butter in a small frying pan. Add the onion and sauté for 5 minutes. Add the spinach and cook until dry. Cool to room temperature.

3. Combine the spinach with the ricotta. Add the eggs and Gruyère cheese and mix well. Season with nutmeg and salt and pepper to taste. If the mixture seems runny, stir in the flour.

4. Spread the filo leaves out, keeping those you are not working with covered with a damp towel.

5. Place one filo leaf in front of you on a clean towel. Brush it with melted butter and sprinkle with a thin layer of bread crumbs. Repeat three more times to make a total of four layers. Do not butter or bread-crumb the top layer. Spread one third of the filling down the length of the filo, 2 inches in from the edge. Fold the 2-inch flap of filo over the stuffing, fold in the sides, and roll up the rest of the dough, using the towel as leverage to pull the roll tight. Put the completed roll on a buttered baking sheet and brush the top of the roll with melted butter. Repeat the entire process two more times with the remaining filo leaves.

6. Preheat the oven to 400 degrees.

7. Bake the rolls for 25 to 30 minutes, or until brown and crisp. Slice and serve warm.

NOTE: The rolls can be prepared to the end of Step 5 and kept in the refrigerator for several hours or overnight. Just cover the rolls with foil before you refrigerate them. Take them out of the refrigerator ½ hour before you plan to bake them and keep them covered until just before you put them in the oven. Spread them with more melted butter before baking.

Jura Cheese Pie

6 TO 8 SERVINGS

1 Basic Quiche Crust (see recipe p. 50)	Salt
	Freshly ground black pepper
2 eggs, beaten	1 tablespoon butter or
3 tablespoons all-purpose flour	margarine
1½ cups heavy cream	¾ cup chopped walnuts
Pinch of ground nutmeg	½ cup grated Gruyère cheese

1. Prepare the Basic Quiche Crust, roll it out, and fit it into a buttered and floured quiche pan. Set it aside.

2. Use a whisk to mix the eggs and the flour together. Add the cream gradually. Season the custard with the nutmeg and salt and pepper to taste.

3. Preheat the oven to 375 degrees.

4. Dot the bottom of the prepared crust with the butter. Sprinkle the walnuts evenly over the butter. Then sprinkle on the cheese. Pour in the prepared custard.

5. Bake for 40 to 45 minutes, or until set. Serve at room temperature.

Guacamole Tart

6 SERVINGS

1½ cups all purpose flour
  Salt
6 tablespoons butter or
  margarine
1 egg yolk
2 to 3 tablespoons cold water
2 ripe avocados
  Juice of 1 lime
1 or 2 canned chilies
½ clove garlic, peeled (optional)

  Juice of 1 lemon
½ to ¾ cup sour cream
2 tablespoons chopped parsley
1 small onion, peeled and
  minced
2 tomatoes, peeled, seeded, and
  diced
3 to 4 ounces Cheddar cheese,
  shredded

1. Put the flour into a bowl with a pinch of salt. Cut in the butter, using a pastry blender or two knives, until the mixture resembles coarse meal. Work in the egg yolk and only enough water to combine the mixture until it leaves the sides of the bowl and forms a ball. Cover the bowl and refrigerate for ½ hour. Then roll the dough out and fit it into a buttered 9-inch tart pan. Prick the crust well with a fork and bake it in a preheated 400-degree oven for 25 minutes, or until it is golden brown.

2. Put the avocado flesh, lime juice, chilies, garlic, and salt to taste in the container of a blender or food processor. Blend until puréed. Transfer to a bowl and cover with a layer of lemon juice to prevent discoloring.

3. Assemble the tart as close to serving time as possible. Drain the lemon juice from the avocado mixture and spread the purée in an even layer on the bottom of the crust. Spread a thin layer of sour cream over the purée to cover it completely.

4. Mound the parsley in the center of the tart. Circle the parsley with a ring of the minced onion. Then make a ring with the diced tomatoes, halfway between the onion ring and the outside crust. End with a ring of shredded Cheddar near the outside crust. Serve immediately.

German Onion Tart

12 SERVINGS

2½ to 3 cups plus 2 tablespoons
  all-purpose flour
Salt
1 teaspoon baking powder
½ cup plus 4 tablespoons butter
  or margarine
2 eggs
½ cup plus 3 tablespoons sour
  cream

4 slices bacon, diced
1½ pounds onions, peeled and
  sliced thin
½ teaspoon caraway seeds
  Freshly ground black pepper
1 egg yolk

1. Put 2½ cups of flour in a bowl with 1 teaspoon of salt and the baking powder. Cut in ½ cup of butter, using a pastry blender or two knives, until the mixture resembles coarse meal. Beat 1 egg and 3 tablespoons sour cream together and work into the dough until it leaves the sides of the bowl and forms a ball. If more flour is needed, add the additional ½ cup. Cover the bowl and refrigerate for ½ hour. Then roll the dough out and fit it into a buttered jelly roll pan, making sure the dough comes up the sides of the pan. Set aside.

2. Melt 4 tablespoons of butter in a large frying pan. Add the bacon, onions, caraway seeds, and salt and pepper to taste. Cover and steam until the onions are very tender.

3. Sprinkle 2 tablespoons of flour over the onions and mix in. Stir ½ cup sour cream, 1 egg, and the egg yolk together and add to the onions. Cook and stir for 3 to 4 minutes. Correct seasonings, if necessary.

4. Preheat the oven to 400 degrees.

5. Pour the onion mixture into the prepared crust and bake for 30 minutes, or until the crust is golden and the onions are browned on top. Serve hot or at room temperature.

NOTE: If you don't have a jelly roll pan, you can use two 9-inch pie pans.

Pissaladière

6 TO 8 SERVINGS

1 Basic Quiche Crust (see recipe p. 50)
6 tablespoons butter, margarine, or oil
Salt
6 large onions, peeled and sliced thin

Pinch of sugar
Freshly ground black pepper
2 tomatoes, cored and sliced
3 tablespoons chopped parsley
Crumbled dried oregano
2 small tins anchovies, drained
Pitted black olives

1. Prepare the Basic Quiche Crust, increasing the salt in the recipe to 1 teaspoon. Roll the dough out after it has chilled and cut out a 9-inch circle of dough. Prick the dough all over with a fork. Bake it on a greased and floured baking sheet in a 400-degree oven for 20 minutes. Remove from the oven but do not turn the oven off.

2. Melt 3 tablespoons of butter in a frying pan. Add the onions and sauté them until they are very soft. Season the onions with sugar and salt and pepper to taste while they are cooking. Spread the cooked onions on the prepared crust.

3. Arrange the sliced tomatoes over the onions. Sprinkle the tomatoes with the parsley and oregano and more salt and pepper.

4. Use the anchovies to form a lattice over the tomatoes. Put a black olive half, cut side down, in the middle of each lattice square. Melt the remaining 3 tablespoons of butter and drizzle it over the top of the pie.

5. Return the pie to the oven and bake for 15 minutes, or until done. Serve hot or warm, sliced in wedges.

Caviar Tart

6 TO 8 SERVINGS

Butter or margarine
12 hard-cooked eggs (see recipe p. 45), peeled
½ cup butter or margarine, melted
Salt
Freshly ground black pepper
1 to 1½ cups sour cream
1 small container red caviar
1 small onion, peeled and minced
1 small container black caviar

1. Butter an 8- or 9-inch springform pan and set aside.

2. Chop, and then mash to a paste, ten of the hard-cooked eggs. Mix them with the melted butter and salt and pepper to taste. Press the egg mixture evenly over the bottom of the prepared springform pan. Spread a layer of sour cream evenly over the eggs. Put in the freezer for about 20 minutes, or until the sour cream has hardened a little.

3. Separate the whites and yolks of the two remaining eggs. Chop the whites finely and sieve the yolks.

4. Take the springform pan out of the freezer and remove the sides of the pan. Make a small circle of the sieved egg yolks in the center of the tart. Around this, place a circle of red caviar. Then circle the red caviar with a ring of finely chopped onion. Then make a ring of black caviar. Make a final ring of the finely chopped egg whites on the outside edge of the tart. Refrigerate until serving time.

NOTE: Some brands of caviar may discolor the sour cream, so assemble the tart as close to serving time as possible.

3
Eggs and Quiches

Avocado Eggs, Caviar Eggs, Tomato Eggs, and Quiche Lorraine.

There are some wonderful dishes here that you are going to enjoy making and eating. I will tell you a very simple way to make an omelet and to poach eggs. And I am sure you will enjoy my variations of the stuffed egg. The quiche recipes, which come at the end of the chapter, make good luncheon dishes that will impress your guests.

Poached Eggs

6 SERVINGS

6 cups water   6 eggs
1 cup red wine vinegar

1. Bring the water and vinegar to a boil in a deep saucepan.
2. Turn down the heat so that the water just simmers. Break the eggs open and ease them into the simmering water one at a time. Simmer for 3 to 5 minutes. (Do not add salt to the poaching liquid because salt tends to break down the structure of the egg.)
3. Remove the eggs with a slotted spoon and drain briefly.

NOTE: The eggs can be poached and kept for reheating later if you poach them for 3 minutes only. Remove the eggs from the poaching liquid, add them to a bowl of cold salted water, and refrigerate them until needed. To warm them, drop the eggs into boiling water for 1 or 2 minutes, or until they are heated through.

Basic Stuffed Eggs

8 SERVINGS

8 hard-cooked eggs, cut in half   Salt
½ cup cream cheese, softened   Freshly ground black pepper

1. Put the yolks of the eggs into a small bowl and mash them with a fork or put them through a ricer. Add the cream cheese and whip until the mixture is very smooth. Season with salt and pepper to taste and whip again.
2. Use a pastry bag with a star-shaped nozzle to pipe the mixture decoratively into the sixteen egg white halves.

Springtime Soufflé

6 SERVINGS

3 pounds fresh spinach, picked
   over and washed
9 tablespoons butter or
   margarine
1 small onion, peeled and
   chopped
3 to 4 anchovy fillets, diced
   Salt
   Freshly ground black pepper
   Ground nutmeg (optional)

3 tablespoons all-purpose flour
1½ cups milk
4 egg yolks
½ cup grated Swiss cheese
¼ cup plus 2 tablespoons grated
   Parmesan cheese
6 poached eggs (see recipe
   p. 41)
5 egg whites

1. Blanch the spinach in boiling salted water. Refresh under cold running water, drain well, squeezing out all the liquid with your hands, and chop it coarsely.

2. Melt 3 tablespoons of butter in a medium-size frying pan. Add the onion and sauté for 5 minutes, or until soft.

3. Add the anchovies and sauté for 2 minutes. Add the spinach and cook for 2 minutes more. Season to taste with salt, pepper, and nutmeg. Set the mixture aside.

4. Melt 3 tablespoons of butter in a small saucepan. Add the flour all at once and stir until the mixture is smooth. Remove from the heat and let the mixture cool a little.

5. Heat the milk and, when it is hot but not boiling, pour it into the cooled *roux*, stirring constantly. Cook over low heat until the mixture is thickened.

6. Remove from the heat and beat in the egg yolks one at a time. Season with salt and pepper to taste. Stir in the Swiss cheese and ¼ cup of the Parmesan cheese. Let the mixture cool.

7. Preheat the oven to 375 degrees.

8. Butter a 1½-quart glass soufflé dish with the remaining 3 tablespoons of butter. Spread the spinach mixture evenly on the bottom of the dish. Use a spoon to make six indentations in the spinach layer. Put 1 poached egg into each hollow.

9. Beat the egg whites until they are stiff and fold them into the

cheese mixture. Pour the sauce over the eggs and spinach and sprinkle the remaining Parmesan cheese on top.

10. Bake for 20 minutes and serve at once.

Eggs Provençale

6 SERVINGS

6 tablespoons butter or margarine
1 large onion, peeled and chopped
1 clove garlic, peeled and minced
4 large mushrooms, sliced

2 tomatoes, skinned, seeded, and diced
2 tablespoons chopped parsley
Salt
Freshly ground black pepper
6 eggs
6 tablespoons heavy cream

1. Melt 4 tablespoons of butter in a medium-size frying pan. Add the onion and sauté until it is soft. Add the garlic, mushrooms, and tomatoes, and cook over medium heat for 5 minutes, stirring occasionally. Remove from the heat and add the parsley and salt and pepper to taste.

2. Preheat the oven to 350 degrees.

3. Butter six individual ramekins with the remaining 2 tablespoons of butter. Divide the tomato mixture evenly among the ramekins. Break 1 egg carefully into each ramekin. Pour 1 tablespoon of cream over each egg.

4. Put the ramekins in a baking pan and carefully pour in enough boiling water to come halfway up the sides of the ramekins. Bake for 8 minutes, or until the eggs are set. Serve at once.

Basic Omelet

1 SERVING

3 eggs
 Pinch of salt

1 to 2 tablespoons butter or
 margarine

1. Beat the eggs and salt together lightly.

2. Heat a small frying pan and, when it is hot, add the butter. When the butter has melted, pour in the beaten eggs.

3. Let the eggs sit for a few seconds. Then use a fork to stir the eggs in a circular motion.

4. Hold the handle of the pan in your other hand and, tilting the pan away from you, shake it back and forth. If you are shaking the pan properly, the eggs will begin to set at the end of the pan opposite the handle.

5. To fold the omelet, loosen its edges with a fork or small spatula. Tilt the pan away from you and give it a few sharp raps on the burner. The far edge of the omelet will move over the side of the pan a little. Lift the edge of the omelet nearest you and fold it over one third of the way. Then fold over the far edge of the omelet so that it looks like an envelope.

6. Hold the serving plate against the edge of the pan, tilt the pan, and turn the omelet out, upside down, onto the plate.

NOTE: The first rule for making omelets is to always use a seasoned pan (see p. 263). You don't have to buy a special omelet pan; any frying pan will do, if it is seasoned. If you don't use a seasoned pan, your eggs will stick and you will get scrambled eggs, not an omelet.

Eggs with Mustard Sauce

6 SERVINGS

3 large, ripe tomatoes
 Salt
6 eggs, poached for 5 minutes
 (see recipe p. 41)
 Lettuce leaves

Mustard Sauce (see recipe
 p. 216)
Chopped hard-cooked egg
 white
Chopped parsley

1. Core the tomatoes and cut them in half. Use a teaspoon to remove the tomato pulp and seeds. Sprinkle the insides of the tomato halves with salt and turn them upside down on a rack to drain.

2. While the tomatoes are draining, poach the eggs for 5 minutes. Drain the eggs and trim them to fit the tomato halves.

3. Line six small serving plates with lettuce leaves. Center the drained tomato shells on the plate and fit a poached egg into each tomato half. Top each serving with an equal portion of the Mustard Sauce, sprinkle with chopped hard-cooked egg white and parsley, and serve cold.

Hard-Cooked Eggs

8 SERVINGS

Boiling salted water

8 eggs at room temperature

1. Carefully lower the eggs into a pot of boiling salted water. Bring the water to a second boil and simmer the eggs for 12 minutes. If the eggs crack, add 1 or 2 tablespoons of vinegar to the water.

2. Put the boiled eggs under cold running water to cool them. Peel when cool. The peeled eggs can be stored in a container of water in the refrigerator if they are not going to be used immediately.

Hangover Breakfast

6 SERVINGS

6 tablespoons butter or
    margarine
½ cup diced onion
3 large potatoes, cooked and
    sliced

½ cup diced ham
6 large eggs, beaten
Salt
Freshly ground black pepper

1. Melt the butter in a large frying pan. When it is hot, add the onion, potatoes, and ham. Sauté, stirring occasionally, for 5 to 6 minutes.

2. Push the mixture to one side of the frying pan. Pour the beaten eggs into the empty side of the pan and let them sit for a few seconds. Then shake the pan back and forth until the eggs are set. The onion mixture will spread itself through the eggs while you are shaking the pan.

3. Turn the eggs over on themselves as you would for an omelet, turn out of the pan, season with salt and pepper to taste, and serve immediately.

Sweet-Tooth Omelet

1 SERVING

2 tablespoons butter or
    margarine
3 eggs, beaten

2 tablespoons of your favorite
    jelly
¼ cup sugar

1. Melt the butter in an omelet pan and pour in the beaten eggs.

2. Let the eggs sit for a few seconds. Then use a fork to stir the eggs in a circular motion.

3. Hold the handle of the pan in your other hand and, tilting the pan away from you, shake it back and forth. If you are shaking the pan properly, the eggs will begin to set at the end of the pan opposite the handle.

4. Loosen the edges of the omelet with a fork or small spatula. Tilt the pan away from you and give it a few sharp raps on the burner. The far edge of the omelet will move over the side of the pan a little.

5. Spread the jelly down the center of the omelet. Lift the edge of omelet nearest you and fold it over one third of the way. Then fold over the far edge of the omelet so that it looks like an envelope.

6. Hold the serving plate against the edge of the pan, tilt the pan, and turn the omelet out, upside down, onto the plate.

7. Sprinkle the sugar on top of the omelet and use a glowing hot metal skewer to make crisscross markings in the sugar.

Avocado Eggs

8 SERVINGS

1 large ripe avocado
1 Basic Stuffed Egg mixture   Salt
   (see recipe p. 41)   Freshly ground black pepper
   Lemon or lime juice   16 egg white halves

1. Peel the avocado and mash three quarters of it. Combine the purée with the Basic Stuffed Egg mixture. Add lemon juice and salt and pepper to taste.

2. Slice the remaining avocado thinly.

3. Pipe the mixture into the egg white halves, filling each only halfway. Put a thin slice of avocado on top of the filling and pipe the remainder of the filling over the avocado.

Caviar Eggs

8 SERVINGS

½ cup heavy cream, whipped
  Red or black caviar
  Dash of lemon juice
1 Basic Stuffed Egg mixture
  (see recipe p. 41)

Salt
Freshly ground black
  pepper
16 egg white halves

1. Fold the whipped cream, caviar to taste, and the lemon juice into the Basic Stuffed Egg mixture. Season with salt and pepper, if necessary.
2. Use a pastry bag with a star-shaped nozzle to pipe the mixture decoratively into the sixteen egg white halves. Garnish each with a dollop of caviar.

Horseradish Eggs

8 SERVINGS

1 Basic Stuffed Egg mixture
  (see recipe p. 41)
4 tablespoons grated fresh
  horseradish

16 egg white halves

1. Season the Basic Stuffed Egg mixture with 2 tablespoons of grated fresh horseradish.
2. Pipe the mixture decoratively into the egg white halves. Distribute the remaining 2 tablespoons of grated horseradish in equal amounts over the top of each stuffed egg.

Pepper Eggs

8 SERVINGS

2 green peppers   Salt
2 teaspoons paprika   Freshly ground black pepper
1 Basic Stuffed Egg mixture   16 egg white halves
  (see recipe p. 41)

1. Roast the peppers in a hot (400-degree) oven for 20 minutes.
2. When the peppers are cool enough to handle, peel and seed them. Purée the peppers in a blender or food processor.
3. Mix the purée with 1 teaspoon of paprika and the Basic Stuffed Egg mixture. Season with salt and pepper, if necessary.
4. Use a pastry bag with a star-shaped nozzle to pipe the mixture decoratively into the sixteen egg white halves. Sprinkle the remaining paprika evenly on top of the stuffed eggs.

Tomato Eggs

8 SERVINGS

2 tomatoes, peeled, seeded, and   Salt
  diced   Freshly ground black pepper
1 Basic Stuffed Egg mixture   16 egg white halves
  (see recipe p. 41)

1. Put the diced tomatoes in a towel and squeeze them to remove all moisture. Reserve sixteen small pieces for decoration. Mix the rest of the tomatoes with the Basic Stuffed Egg mixture. Season with salt and pepper, if necessary.
2. Pipe the mixture decoratively into the egg white halves. Garnish each with a piece of diced tomato.

Basic Quiche Crust

1½ cups all-purpose flour   2 to 3 tablespoons ice water
    Pinch of salt
½ cup butter or margarine,
    chilled

Combine the flour and salt in a mixing bowl. Cut in the butter, using a pastry blender or two knives, until the mixture resembles coarse meal. Add only enough water to combine the mixture until it leaves the sides of the bowl and forms a ball. Work quickly and do not overwork the dough. Cover the bowl and refrigerate the pastry for ½ hour.

Quiche Lorraine

6 SERVINGS

1 Basic Quiche Crust (see recipe   1 cup heavy cream
    above)   2 tablespoons chopped parsley
¼ pound bacon, diced   Salt
¾ cup grated Swiss cheese   Freshly ground black pepper
4 eggs

1. Prepare the Basic Quiche Crust, roll it out, and fit it into a buttered quiche pan. Prick the crust well with a fork.
2. Sauté the bacon until crisp. Drain it well. Sprinkle the bacon and cheese evenly over the bottom of the quiche crust and press them down lightly.
3. Preheat the oven to 400 degrees.
4. Beat the eggs with the cream until thoroughly blended. Add the parsley and salt and pepper to taste. Pour the mixture over the bacon and cheese.
5. Bake for 25 minutes, or until the crust is done and the filling is set and golden. Serve hot.

Ham and Leek Quiche

6 SERVINGS

1 Basic Quiche Crust (see
    recipe p. 50)
4 leeks, white part only
3 tablespoons butter or
    margarine

Salt
Freshly ground black pepper
⅔ cup diced boiled ham
3 eggs
1½ cups heavy cream

1. Prepare the Basic Quiche Crust, roll it out, and fit it into a buttered quiche pan. Prick the crust well with a fork.

2. Wash the leeks well, cut them into small slices, and drain them thoroughly.

3. Melt the butter in a small frying pan. When it is hot, add the leeks and sauté them for 3 to 4 minutes. Season the leeks with salt and pepper to taste. When the leeks begin to get tender, add the ham and sauté for 2 to 3 minutes longer. Remove from the heat and let cool a little.

4. Preheat the oven to 400 degrees.

5. Beat the eggs with the cream until thoroughly blended. Stir in the leek mixture and correct the seasonings, if necessary. Pour the mixture into the prepared crust.

6. Bake for 25 minutes, or until the crust is done and the filling is set and golden. Serve warm.

Seafood Quiche

6 SERVINGS

1 Basic Quiche Crust (see recipe p. 50)
3 tablespoons butter or margarine
1 cup diced assorted seafood, such as lobster, shrimp, scallops, or sole

¼ cup dry white wine
3 eggs
½ cup heavy cream
2 tablespoons chopped parsley
Salt
Freshly ground black pepper

1. Preheat the oven to 400 degrees.

2. Prepare the Basic Quiche Crust, roll it out, and fit it into a buttered and floured quiche pan. Spread a layer of dried beans over the bottom of the crust to hold the pastry in place. Bake for 15 minutes. Remove from the oven but do not turn the oven off. Remove and discard the beans and set the partially cooked crust aside.

3. Melt the butter in a small frying pan. When it is hot, add the seafood and sauté for 2 minutes. Add the wine and cook over medium-high heat until the wine has almost evaporated. Remove from the heat and let the mixture cool.

4. Beat the eggs with the cream until thoroughly blended. Stir in the seafood mixture and parsley and season with salt and pepper to taste. Pour the mixture into the partially baked crust.

5. Bake for 30 minutes, or until the crust is done and the filling is set and golden. Serve warm.

Shrimp Quiche

6 SERVINGS

1 Basic Quiche Crust (see recipe p. 50)
1 to 2 celery stalks, trimmed and washed
1 carrot, trimmed and scraped
1 medium-size onion, peeled
Salt

1 bay leaf
1 pound unshelled shrimp
3 eggs
1¼ cups heavy cream
Freshly ground black pepper
½ cup grated Swiss cheese

1. Preheat the oven to 375 degrees.

2. Prepare the Basic Quiche Crust, roll it out, and fit it into a buttered and floured quiche pan. Spread a layer of dried beans over the bottom of the crust to hold the pastry in place. Bake for 15 minutes. Remove from the oven. Remove and discard the beans and set the partially cooked crust aside.

3. Chop the celery, carrot, and onion coarsely. Put the vegetables into a medium-size stockpot and add enough water to cover them by 1 inch. Add ½ teaspoon salt and the bay leaf and bring to a boil. Simmer for 15 minutes, add the shrimp, and simmer for 2 to 3 minutes, or until the shrimp turn pink.

4. Remove the shrimp using a slotted spoon. Let them cool and drain. Shell the shrimp, but leave the tails on about twelve of them. Arrange the shrimp with the tails around the edge of the partially cooked pastry so that the tails curl over the top edge of the pastry shell. Dice the remaining shrimp and scatter them over the bottom of the crust.

5. Preheat the oven to 375 degrees.

6. Beat the eggs with the cream until thoroughly blended. Season with salt and pepper to taste and pour the mixture over the shrimp. Sprinkle the grated cheese over the custard.

7. Bake for 30 minutes, or until the filling is set and golden. Serve warm.

Zucchini Quiche

6 SERVINGS

7 medium-size zucchini
　Salt
1 Basic Quiche Crust (see recipe
　p. 50)
2 tablespoons butter or
　margarine
2 eggs

1 egg yolk
1 cup heavy cream
1 heaping teaspoon dried
　marjoram
　Pinch of ground nutmeg
　Freshly ground black pepper

1. Wash and trim, but do not peel, the zucchini. Put them through the julienne blade of a food processor or grate them on a large-holed grater. Put the zucchini in a bowl in layers, salting each layer. Let sit for 30 minutes, then squeeze out the moisture thoroughly. Set the zucchini aside.

2. Preheat the oven to 400 degrees.

3. Prepare the Basic Quiche Crust, roll it out, and fit it into a buttered quiche pan. Spread a layer of dried beans over the bottom of the crust to hold the pastry in place. Bake for 15 minutes. Remove from the oven but do not turn off the oven. Remove and discard the beans and set the partially cooked crust aside.

4. Melt the butter in a small frying pan. When the butter is hot, add the zucchini and sauté for 3 to 4 minutes, or until the zucchini are dry.

5. Beat the eggs, egg yolk, and cream together until thoroughly blended. Stir in the zucchini, marjoram, nutmeg, and salt and pepper to taste. Pour the mixture into the partially baked crust.

6. Bake for 35 minutes, or until the filling is set and golden. Let sit for a few minutes before serving.

4
Stocks and Soups

Cold Broccoli Soup and Gazpacho.

You should try to keep a supply of stock on hand in your refrigerator or freezer. I have simplified stock-making so that it takes only a few hours—and you don't have to stand over it as it cooks, you can go do other things while it simmers. If you have stock on hand, you will be able to make your soups and sauces instantly.

I have given you a good variety of soups here: some thick soups that are just perfect for cold winter days, some delicate cream soups, which won't fill you up too much, and, of course, a few cold soups for those hot summer days.

Beef Stock

ABOUT 1½ QUARTS

3 to 4 pounds assorted beef
    bones and meat, cut up
2 carrots, trimmed and
    chopped
2 celery stalks, trimmed and
    chopped
2 onions, peeled and chopped
2 to 3 tomatoes, cored, peeled,
    and chopped

1 bay leaf
3 parsley sprigs
    Pinch of dried thyme
    Salt to taste
    Freshly ground black pepper
    to taste
12 cups water

1. Put all the ingredients into a large stockpot. Bring to a boil, and simmer, partially covered, for 3 to 4 hours. Skim off any scum that rises to the top.

2. Strain the stock into a large bowl and discard the solids. Cool the stock, chill it, and remove the fat that rises to the top.

Clarified Beef Stock

ABOUT 1½ QUARTS

1½ quarts cooled Beef Stock (see
    recipe above)
¼ pound lean ground beef
1 carrot, trimmed and chopped
1 onion, peeled and chopped
1 leek, washed well and
    chopped
1 celery stalk, trimmed and
    chopped

2 tomatoes, cored, peeled, and
    chopped
2 egg whites
    Shells of 2 eggs (optional)
1 bay leaf
3 parsley sprigs
    Pinch of dried thyme

1. Pour the cool stock into a large stockpot. Mix all the other ingredients together and add to the stock, stirring to mix thoroughly.

2. Bring the stock to a boil over very low heat. The egg whites and shells will form a crust on top of the stock. When this happens, strain the stock through a sieve lined with a damp cloth into a large bowl. Discard any solids and cool and chill the stock.

Veal Stock

ABOUT 1½ QUARTS

3 to 4 pounds veal bones and meat, cut up
2 carrots, trimmed and chopped
2 celery stalks, trimmed and chopped
1 onion, peeled and chopped
1 to 2 cloves garlic, peeled and chopped

1 bay leaf
3 parsley sprigs
  Pinch of dried thyme
  Salt to taste
  Freshly ground black pepper to taste
12 cups water

1. Put all the ingredients in a large stockpot. Bring to a boil and simmer, partially covered, for 3 to 4 hours. Skim off any scum that rises to the top.

2. Strain the stock into a large bowl and discard the solids. Cool the stock, chill it, and remove the fat that rises to the top.

Chicken Stock

ABOUT 1½ QUARTS

2 to 3 pounds meaty chicken
  bones and giblets (not the
  liver)
1 to 2 carrots, trimmed and
  chopped
1 to 2 celery stalks, trimmed
  and chopped
1 onion, peeled and chopped

3 parsley sprigs
1 bay leaf
  Pinch of dried thyme
  Salt to taste
  Freshly ground black pepper
    to taste
12 cups water

1. Put all the ingredients into a large stockpot. Bring to a boil and simmer, partially covered, for 2 to 3 hours. Skim off any scum that rises to the top.

2. Strain the stock into a large bowl and discard the solids. Cool the stock, chill it, and remove the fat that rises to the top.

Fish Stock

ABOUT 1½ QUARTS

3 pounds or more fish bones
  and heads of nonoily
  white-fleshed fish
2 carrots, trimmed and
  chopped
1 celery stalk, trimmed and
  chopped
1 onion, peeled and chopped
1 bay leaf

3 parsley sprigs
  Pinch of dried thyme
  Pinch of fennel seeds
    (optional)
  Salt to taste
  Fresh ground black pepper to
    taste
1 to 2 cups dry white wine
10 cups water

1. Put all the ingredients into a large stockpot. Bring to a boil and simmer, partially covered, for 30 to 45 minutes. Remove the scum as it rises to the top.

2. Strain the stock into a large bowl and discard the solids. Cool the stock, chill it, and remove the fat, if any, that rises to the top.

NOTE: If you want a more concentrated flavor, return the strained stock to a clean pan and reduce it, over medium-high heat, until it is half the original amount.

Consommé Royale

6 SERVINGS

1 egg
2 egg yolks
⅔ cup heavy cream
  Salt

Freshly ground black pepper
Pinch of ground nutmeg
6 cups Clarified Beef Stock (see
  recipe p. 56)

1. Preheat the oven to 350 degrees.

2. Put the egg, egg yolks, cream, salt and pepper to taste, and nutmeg into a small bowl and beat until very well combined. Pour the mixture into a greased 2-cup soufflé dish.

3. Set the dish into a larger baking pan and pour in enough boiling water to come halfway up the sides of the soufflé dish. Bake for 25 minutes, or until set. Remove from the oven and take the soufflé dish out of the baking pan. Cool, unmold, and cut into small cubes.

4. To assemble the soup, heat the stock, put the cubes of royale in the bottom of the soup bowls, and pour the hot stock over them. Serve immediately.

Russian Borscht

6 SERVINGS

3 tablespoons vegetable oil
1 onion, peeled and chopped
2 leeks, well washed and
   chopped
2 pounds diced meat (a
   combination of beef, pork,
   duck, chicken or goose)
   Salt
   Freshly ground black pepper
1 bay leaf

½ head green cabbage, cored and
   chopped
2 carrots, trimmed, scraped, and
   chopped
3 turnips, peeled and diced
2 potatoes, peeled and diced
   Water
1 to 2 cups sour cream
1 8-ounce can sliced pickled
   beets, drained

1. Heat the oil in a large saucepan. When it is hot, add the onion and leeks and sauté for 5 minutes, stirring occasionally. Add the diced meats and season with salt and pepper to taste. Cook for 20 minutes, stirring occasionally.

2. Add the bay leaf, cabbage, carrots, turnips, and potatoes and stir well. Add water to cover the vegetables by 3 inches, bring to a boil, cover, and simmer for 45 minutes, or until the vegetables are tender.

3. Add some of the hot stock from the soup to the sour cream to liquefy it. Stir the sour cream into the soup, add the beets, and serve immediately.

Hungarian Goulash Soup

6 SERVINGS

3 tablespoons vegetable oil
1 pound chuck, flank, or bottom round, diced
2 pounds onions, peeled and diced
2 cloves garlic, peeled and minced
1 cup tomato purée
2 tablespoons paprika
1 tablespoon Goulash Spice (see recipe p. 204)
2 cups peeled and diced potatoes
1 green pepper, seeded and diced
1 cup washed and drained sauerkraut
Water
Salt
Freshly ground black pepper

1. Heat the oil in a 4-quart pot. Add the meat and sauté for 5 minutes, stirring to separate the pieces. Add the onions and cook until they are golden brown. Add the garlic, tomato purée, paprika, and Goulash Spice. Stir well and add water to cover the ingredients by 3 inches.

2. Bring to a boil and add the potatoes, green pepper, and sauerkraut. Bring to a boil again, cover, lower the heat, and simmer for 1½ to 2 hours. Season with salt and pepper to taste. Serve the soup with bread.

Scotch Barley Soup

6 SERVINGS

¾ pound shoulder lamb with bones
3 quarts water
2 leeks, washed well and julienned
6 trimmed and scraped carrots (2 whole, 4 diced)
6 trimmed celery stalks (2 whole, 4 diced)
2 large onions, peeled (1 whole, 1 diced)
1 bay leaf
3 cloves garlic, peeled and mashed
Salt
Freshly ground black pepper
1 tablespoon vegetable oil
½ cup pearl barley, washed and drained
½ cup heavy cream or half-and-half
½ cup chopped parsley

1. Cut most of the meat from the bones and dice it. Set the meat aside in a bowl in the refrigerator.

2. Heat the water, add the bones and any meat scraps, the green part of the leeks, 2 carrots, 2 celery stalks, the whole onion, bay leaf, garlic, and salt and pepper to taste. Bring to a boil, lower the heat, and simmer for 1 hour. Skim off any scum that rises to the top. Strain the stock through a sieve into a large bowl. Discard the solids and set the stock aside.

3. Clean out the stockpot you used to make the lamb stock and add the oil to it. When the oil is hot, add the reserved lamb cubes. Brown them on all sides and add the diced carrots, celery, onion, and white part of leeks. Sauté for 3 to 4 minutes stirring occasionally. Add the barley and strained stock. Bring to a boil, lower the heat, and simmer for 40 to 50 minutes.

4. Remove from the heat and add the cream. Serve each portion sprinkled with parsley.

Carrots and Cream Soup

6 SERVINGS

1 pound carrots	Salt
3 tablespoons butter or margarine	Freshly ground black pepper
	Pinch of sugar
4 tablespoons all-purpose flour	3 egg yolks
½ cup chopped onion	¾ cup heavy cream
8 cups Chicken Stock (see recipe p. 58)	

1. Trim and scrape the carrots. Reserve 2 for garnish and dice the rest.

2. Melt the butter in a large saucepan. Add the flour all at once and stir to make a smooth, creamy mixture. Add the chopped onion and the diced carrots. Stir and cook over low heat for 3 to 4 minutes. Remove from the heat and let the mixture cool a little.

3. Heat the stock and slowly add it to the cooled carrot mixture, stirring constantly. Bring the soup to a simmer and let it simmer for 45 minutes.

4. Purée the soup in a blender or food processor and season with salt and pepper to taste.

5. Julienne the two remaining carrots (see p. 5) and cook them in boiling salted water to which you have added the pinch of sugar until they are barely tender. Refresh under cold water, drain, and set aside.

6. Beat the egg yolks with the cream. Add to the hot soup while stirring. Add the julienned carrots to heat them through and serve immediately.

NOTE: The soup can be prepared to the end of Step 5 and refrigerated. Right before serving, just bring it to the boiling point and continue with Step 6. Do not reboil the soup after the egg yolks and cream have been added.

Cauliflower and Cream Soup

6 SERVINGS

3 quarts water
Juice of 1 lemon
1 head cauliflower
½ cup butter or margarine
½ cup all-purpose flour

½ cup minced onion
Salt
Freshly ground black pepper
½ cup heavy cream
2 egg yolks

1. Heat the water and add the lemon juice. Add the whole head of cauliflower and cook for about 10 minutes, or until just barely tender.

2. Remove the cauliflower, reserving the liquid, and cut off the green leaves and shred them. Break the cauliflower into flowerets and set them aside.

3. Melt the butter and add the flour all at once, stirring to make a smooth, creamy mixture. Add the shredded cauliflower leaves and the onion and cook for 3 to 4 minutes, stirring occasionally. Let the mixture cool. When cool, slowly add the cauliflower poaching liquid. Bring to a simmer and cook for ½ hour. Season with salt and pepper to taste.

4. Strain the soup through a sieve into another pot. Keep it warm over very low heat.

5. Beat the cream and egg yolks together and add to the hot soup, stirring until thickened. Serve the soup garnished with the cauliflower flowerets.

Potage Freneuse

6 SERVINGS

6 tablespoons butter or
   margarine
1 pound white turnips, peeled
   and sliced thin
2 large potatoes, peeled and
   sliced thin
   Salt

Freshly ground black pepper
4 cups Chicken Stock (see recipe
   p. 58)
1 cup heavy cream
   Garlic Croutons (see recipe
   p. 159)

1. Melt 3 tablespoons of butter in a large heavy pot. Add the turnips and the potatoes, season with salt and pepper to taste, cover, and cook, stirring occasionally, until the vegetables are soft. You want to steam the vegetables, not let them brown. If they start to stick, add a little stock.

2. When the turnips and potatoes are soft, add the stock and cook for 20 minutes. The total cooking time for the vegetables will be 35 to 40 minutes.

3. Purée the soup through a food mill or in a blender or food processor. Add the cream and reheat the soup, stirring in the remaining butter. Serve hot with Croutons.

NOTE: The soup can be prepared ahead to the point of puréeing it. It can then be refrigerated and reheated before the butter is added.

French Onion Soup

6 SERVINGS

5 tablespoons butter or
    margarine
3 cups thinly sliced onions
½ cup dry white wine (optional)
1 clove garlic, minced
   Salt
   Freshly ground black pepper

3 cups Beef or Chicken Stock
    (see recipes pp. 56 and 58)
1 cup Garlic Croutons (see
    recipe p. 159)
½ cup grated Parmesan cheese
½ cup grated Gruyère cheese

    1. Melt 3 tablespoons of butter in a heavy saucepan and add the onions. Sauté over low heat until golden. Add the white wine, garlic, and salt and pepper to taste. Cook for a few minutes to reduce the wine by half. Add the stock, stir well, and cook for 20 to 30 minutes.
    2. Preheat the oven to 350 degrees.
    3. Pour the soup into individual ramekins and top each serving with Croutons. Mix the cheeses together and sprinkle them evenly over the Croutons. Dot each serving evenly with the remaining butter and bake until the cheese is golden brown. Serve immediately.

Potato Soup

6 SERVINGS

3 tablespoons butter or
    margarine
½ cup minced onion
1 pound leeks, washed well and
    sliced
2 pounds potatoes, peeled and
    sliced
6 cups Chicken Stock (see
    recipe p. 58)

   Salt
   Freshly ground black pepper
4 egg yolks
2 cups heavy cream
   Dried marjoram
½ cup chopped parsley
   Garlic Croutons (see recipe
    p. 159)

1. Melt the butter in a large saucepan. Add the onion and leeks and sauté for 5 minutes, or until they are soft. Add the potatoes, stock, and salt and pepper to taste. Simmer until the potatoes are tender, about 15 minutes.

2. Purée the soup through a food mill or in a blender or food processor. Return the soup to the saucepan and keep it warm over very low heat.

3. Beat the egg yolks and cream together and stir the mixture into the soup. Correct the seasonings, if necessary. Serve the soup hot, garnished with marjoram, parsley, and Croutons.

Cream of Tomato Soup

6 SERVINGS

1 tablespoon olive oil
2 tablespoons butter or margarine
1 large onion, peeled and chopped
4 large tomatoes, cored and cut into eighths, but not peeled or seeded
3 tablespoons tomato paste
Pinch of dried thyme
1 clove garlic, peeled and crushed
¼ cup all-purpose flour
3 cups Chicken Stock (see recipe p. 58)
2 cups water
Salt
Freshly ground black pepper
Dash of sugar
1 cup heavy cream

1. Heat the oil and butter together in a deep saucepan. Add the onion and sauté until it is limp. Add the tomatoes and tomato paste and cook for 5 minutes, stirring occasionally. Add the thyme and garlic. Stir in the flour and mix well. Add the stock, water, salt and pepper to taste, and the sugar. Simmer for 30 minutes.

2. Purée the soup through a food mill or in a blender and then pass it through a sieve to remove any seeds.

3. Return the soup to a clean pan and add the cream. Correct seasonings, if necessary. Heat gently, but do not boil. The soup can also be served cold.

Agnès Sorel Soup

6 SERVINGS

8 cups Chicken Stock (see recipe p. 58)
1 whole chicken
1 bay leaf
4 tablespoons butter or margarine
4 tablespoons all-purpose flour
2 celery stalks, trimmed and chopped

1 onion, peeled and chopped
3 leeks (white part only), washed well and chopped
1 cup heavy cream
Salt
Freshly ground black pepper
1 can white asparagus tips

1. Put the stock, the whole chicken, and the bay leaf into a large pot. Bring to a boil, cover, lower the heat, and poach the chicken for 35 to 45 minutes, or until tender. Remove the chicken and bay leaf from the stock. Discard the bay leaf and let the chicken cool until it is cool enough to handle.

2. While the chicken is cooling, melt the butter in a large saucepan and add the flour all at once, stirring to make a smooth, creamy mixture. Add the celery, onion, and leeks. Stir and cook for 3 to 4 minutes. Remove from the heat and let cool.

3. Skin and bone the chicken and dice the meat.

4. Heat 6 cups of the stock in which the chicken was poached. Add the hot stock to the cooled vegetable mixture, stirring constantly. Bring the soup to a simmer, and cook until the vegetables are tender, 20 to 25 minutes.

5. Strain the soup into a clean pot. Add the cream and salt and pepper to taste. Add the diced chicken and asparagus and heat through. Serve hot.

Cold Broccoli Soup

6 SERVINGS

2 bunches fresh broccoli, washed
    and drained
2 cups water

2 cups heavy cream
Salt
Freshly ground black pepper

1. Cut the stalks off the broccoli and peel them. Slice the stalks into ¼-inch-thick slices and put the slices into a saucepan. Break the broccoli heads into flowerets and add them to the stalks. Add the water to the saucepan and bring to a boil. Cover, lower the heat, and cook for 8 to 10 minutes.

2. Set aside twelve broccoli flowerets for garnish. Purée the rest of the broccoli and the cooking liquid with a food mill or in a blender or food processor. Stir in the cream and add salt and pepper to taste. Chill the soup, covered, in the refrigerator. Serve cold garnished with the reserved flowerets.

Cucumber-Dill Soup

6 SERVINGS

3 cucumbers, peeled and
    chopped
1 clove garlic, peeled
1 cup plain yogurt

1 cup sour cream
2 tablespoons chopped dill
Salt
Freshly ground black pepper

1. Put the cucumbers, garlic, yogurt, sour cream, and 1 tablespoon of the dill into the container of a food processor or blender. Purée well and season with salt and pepper to taste. Cover and chill in the refrigerator.

2. Serve the soup in chilled bowls and garnish each serving with a little of the remaining dill.

Cream of Curry Soup

6 SERVINGS

4 tablespoons butter or
  margarine
4 tablespoons all-purpose flour
1 onion, peeled and chopped
1 apple, peeled, cored, and
  chopped
4 cups Chicken Stock (see
  recipe p. 58)
½ cup mango chutney
1 tablespoon curry powder

Salt
Freshly ground black pepper
Pinch of ground coriander
1 cup half-and-half
1 cup heavy cream
½ cup diced green pepper
½ cup diced red pepper
½ cup diced and peeled mango
½ cup toasted sliced almonds

1. Melt the butter in a saucepan and add the flour all at once, stirring to make a smooth, creamy mixture. Add the onion and apple and cook, stirring, for 4 to 5 minutes. Remove from the heat and let cool.

2. Heat the Chicken Stock.

3. Add the chutney and curry powder to the onion-apple mixture. Slowly add the hot stock, stirring constantly. Season with salt and pepper to taste and the ground coriander. Bring to a simmer and cook for 45 minutes. Strain the soup, discarding the solids, and refrigerate, covered, until cold.

4. At serving time, add the half-and-half and heavy cream to the soup. Correct the seasonings, if necessary. Garnish each serving with a little of the peppers, mango, and almonds.

Gazpacho

6 SERVINGS

Soup:

2 cups tomato juice
1 large cucumber, peeled and
  diced
2 small onions, peeled and
  chopped
2 whole tomatoes, peeled,
  seeded, and diced
1 large green pepper, seeded
  and diced
2 cloves garlic

½ cup wine vinegar
½ cup olive oil
  Juice of 1 lemon
2 eggs
½ cup half-and-half
  Salt to taste
  Freshly ground black pepper
    to taste
  Dash of Tabasco sauce

Garnish:

Chopped parsley
Diced tomato
Chopped cucumber

Chopped red and green
  peppers

1. Put all the soup ingredients in a blender or food processor and
purée until smooth. Cover and refrigerate until cold.
2. Serve from a soup tureen, with the garnishes on the side. Let
each person garnish his or her own serving.

Vichyssoise

6 SERVINGS

3 to 4 leeks (white part only), washed well and sliced
1 onion, peeled and diced
4 large potatoes, peeled and sliced
4 cups Chicken Stock (see recipe p. 58)
1 bay leaf
Salt
Freshly ground black pepper
2 cups half-and-half
1 cup heavy cream
Chopped parsley or scallions for garnish

1. Combine the leeks, onion, potatoes, and stock in a saucepan. Add the cloves, bay leaf, and salt and pepper to taste. Bring to a boil, cover, and lower the heat. Simmer for 30 minutes, or until the vegetables are tender. Remove the cloves and bay leaf. Cool the soup and purée it in a blender or food processor. Refrigerate, covered, overnight.
2. When ready to serve, stir in the half-and-half and heavy cream. Correct the seasonings, if necessary. Serve ice cold, garnished with parsley or scallions.

Cold Zucchini Soup

6 TO 8 SERVINGS

2 pounds zucchini
3 cups Chicken Stock (see recipe p. 58)
1 teaspoon dried marjoram
2 tablespoons butter or margarine
2 tablespoons all-purpose flour
2 cups milk
Salt
Freshly ground black pepper
1 cup heavy cream
Chopped parsley for garnish

1. Trim, wash, and slice the zucchini. Put in a saucepan with the stock and marjoram. Cook until tender, about 20 minutes. Purée through a food mill or in a blender or food processor.

2. Melt the butter and add the flour all at once, stirring to make a smooth, creamy mixture. Cook, stirring, for 2 to 3 minutes, and remove from the heat. Cool slightly.

3. Heat the milk until it just comes to a boil. Add the milk to the cooled *roux*. Return to the heat and cook, stirring, for 15 minutes, or until the floury taste is gone. Add the puréed zucchini and season with salt and pepper to taste. Chill thoroughly.

4. Stir the cream into the chilled soup. Correct the seasonings, if necessary. Serve garnished with chopped parsley.

5

Meats

Roast Pork with Prunes and Beef Rouladen.

You don't have to use very expensive cuts of meat to make good main dishes, as you will see from the following recipes. It's always helpful, of course, to have a supply of meat in your freezer—which you have wisely bought on sale. This will cut costs and make you feel good about your food bills.

Sauerbraten

6 SERVINGS

Salt
Freshly ground black pepper
1 4-pound top or bottom round
   roast beef
2 carrots, trimmed, scraped,
   and diced
2 celery stalks, trimmed and
   diced

2 bay leaves
2 cloves garlic, peeled
1½ cups dry red wine
1½ cups red wine vinegar
2 cups water
3 tablespoons butter or
   margarine

1. Season the meat with salt and pepper. Combine all the other ingredients except the butter in a glass or ceramic bowl. Add the seasoned meat, cover, and refrigerate for 4 to 5 days. Turn the meat twice a day while it is marinating.

2. When you are ready to cook the meat, melt the butter in an ovenproof pot, remove the meat from the marinade, and brown the meat on all sides in the hot butter.

3. Preheat the oven to 325 degrees.

4. Strain the marinade over the browned beef, cover the pot, and bake for 2½ to 3 hours, or until the meat is tender.

Brisket with Potatoes

6 TO 8 SERVINGS

1 5- to 6-pound brisket
2 pounds beef soup bones
   Water
3 tablespoons butter, margarine,
      or oil
1 leek, washed well and chopped
1 onion, peeled and chopped
1 carrot, trimmed, scraped, and
      chopped

1 celery stalk, trimmed and
      chopped
2 cloves garlic, peeled
4 potatoes, peeled and diced
1 bay leaf
3 parsley sprigs
   Salt
   Freshly ground black pepper

1. Put the brisket and the bones into a deep pot. Add water to cover by 2 inches. Bring to a boil, lower the heat, and simmer for 1½ hours, or until the meat is barely tender. Skim off any scum that rises to the top. Remove the cooked brisket from the pot and let it drain. Remove the bones from the stock and discard them.

2. Melt the butter in an ovenproof pot. Add the leek, onion, carrot, and celery. Sauté, stirring, for 5 minutes. Add the garlic, potatoes, bay leaf, and parsley sprigs. Season with salt and pepper to taste. Pour in enough of the stock in which the brisket was cooked to barely cover the vegetables.

3. Preheat the oven to 400 degrees.

4. Push the vegetables to the sides of the pot and nestle the brisket down in the center of the pot. Bake for 45 minutes, or until everything is tender. Slice and serve the meat with the vegetables and Horseradish Sauce (see recipe p. 216).

Braised Beef

6 SERVINGS

2 tablespoons butter or
    margarine
1½ to 2 pounds top or bottom
    round in one piece
1 cup chopped carrot
1 cup chopped celery

1 cup dry red wine
1 cup water
4 tablespoons tomato purée
Salt
Freshly ground black pepper

1. Preheat the oven to 375 degrees.
2. Melt the butter in a heavy ovenproof pot. Add the beef and brown on both sides. Remove the beef to a plate and add the vegetables to the pot. Sauté them gently for about 5 minutes. Add the wine, water, and purée to the vegetables and stir in well. Season with salt and pepper to taste. Return the meat to the pot, cover, and bake for 45 minutes to 1 hour.

German Beef and Vegetable Stew

6 SERVINGS

6 tablespoons vegetable oil
2 pounds boneless beef, cubed
Salt
Freshly ground black pepper
1 onion, peeled and sliced
1 cup julienned carrots
½ cup julienned leeks

1 cup julienned celery
2 potatoes, peeled and diced
3 cups Beef or Chicken Stock
    (see recipes pp. 56 and 58)
12 ounces noodles, cooked in
    boiling salted water

1. Heat the oil in a large heavy pot and add the beef. Sauté for 5 minutes, turning the beef until it is brown on all sides. Season with salt and pepper to taste.
2. Add the vegetables and sauté for 5 minutes longer. Add the stock and simmer for 30 to 35 minutes, or until the meat is tender.
3. When you are ready to serve the stew, add the cooked noodles to the pot and combine them well with the vegetables and meat.

Beef Rouladen

6 SERVINGS

6 tablespoons butter, margarine, or vegetable oil
2 onions, peeled and chopped
6 slices top round
  Salt
  Freshly ground black pepper
2 tablespoons Dijon mustard
2 tablespoons chopped Kosher dill pickles or cornichons
1 slice raw bacon, diced

1 carrot, trimmed, scraped, and chopped
1 celery stalk, trimmed and chopped
2 cups Beef Stock (see recipe p. 56)
1 cup dry red wine
1 tablespoon cornstarch
2 tablespoons cold water

1. Melt 2 tablespoons of butter in a small frying pan. Add 1 chopped onion and sauté for 5 minutes, or until golden. Remove from the heat.

2. Pound the meat lightly and sprinkle the pieces with salt and pepper. Spread the mustard on one side of each slice of meat. Distribute the sautéed onion, pickles, and diced bacon equally among the slices of meat. Roll the beef slices up and hold closed with toothpicks.

3. Melt the remaining butter in a frying pan large enough to hold the Rouladen in one layer. When it is hot, add the beef rolls and sauté them on all sides until they are browned. Add the remaining onion, the carrot, and the celery to the pan. Stir and brown a little. Add the stock and wine and mix well. Cover the pan and cook over low heat for 45 minutes to 1 hour, or until the meat is tender.

4. Remove the meat to a plate and keep warm. Strain the sauce and discard the vegetables. Return the strained sauce to the pan over low heat. Combine the cornstarch and water to make a thin paste. Slowly add the mixture to the sauce, stirring constantly until the sauce thickens. Return the meat rolls to the frying pan and coat them with sauce. Serve immediately.

Strindberg Steak

6 SERVINGS

6 small steaks, such as
   tenderloin steaks
Salt
Coarsely ground black
   pepper
6 tablespoons Dijon mustard
1 large onion, peeled and
   minced

Flour for dredging
4 tablespoons vegetable oil
1½ cups dry red wine
1½ cups Demi-Glace (see recipe
   p. 206) or Beef Stock (see
   recipe p. 56)

1. Pound the steaks lightly with a flat mallet. Season them well with salt and pepper. Score on side of the steaks with a knife to form a diamond pattern.

2. Spread 1 tablespoon of mustard on each steak. Press the chopped onion evenly on top of the mustard. Use the palm of your hand to press the onion into place on each steak.

3. Dredge the steaks in flour, being careful to leave the onion coating on the steaks.

4. Heat the oil in a large frying pan. When it is almost smoking, add the steaks, onion side down. Sauté quickly to the desired degree of doneness. Remove the meat to a serving platter and keep it warm.

5. Pour the wine and Demi-Glace into the pan and stir with a wooden spoon to incorporate any browned-on bits in the pan. Cook for 2 or 3 minutes over high heat and pour the sauce over the steaks. Serve immediately.

Hungarian Goulash I

6 SERVINGS

3 tablespoons vegetable oil
1½ to 2 pounds chuck, bottom
    round, or flank steak,
    cubed
1½ pounds onions, peeled and
    sliced
3 tablespoons tomato purée
1½ pounds sauerkraut, washed
    and drained
3 teaspoons paprika
1 large potato, peeled and cut
    into ¼-inch dice

4 cloves garlic
1 bay leaf
    Pinch of caraway seeds
    Pinch of dried marjoram
    Peel of 1 lemon
    Salt
    Freshly ground black pepper
1½ cups Beef Stock (see recipe p.
    56) or water

1. Preheat the oven to 400 degrees.

2. Heat the oil in an ovenproof pot. Add the meat and sauté, stirring occasionally, until the meat is brown. Add the onions and tomato purée and sauté for 5 minutes longer. Add the sauerkraut, paprika, and potato and mix in well. Add the garlic, bay leaf, caraway seeds, marjoram, lemon peel, and salt and pepper to taste. Mix well and pour in the stock. Cover and bake for 45 to 50 minutes, or until the meat is tender. If the dish gets too dry, add more stock or water during the cooking.

Hungarian Goulash II

6 SERVINGS

4 tablespoons vegetable oil
2½ pounds boneless beef, cubed
2 tablespoons butter or
    margarine
1 large onion, peeled and sliced
2 cloves garlic, peeled and
    crushed

2 tablespoons paprika
½ cup tomato purée
    Salt
    Freshly ground black pepper
2 tablespoons all-purpose flour
2 cups Beef Stock (see recipe
    p. 56)

1. Heat the oil in a frying pan. When hot, add the beef and sauté until it is brown on all sides. Remove the beef and set it aside.

2. Melt the butter in a large heavy pot. Add the onion and sauté until it is golden. Add the garlic, paprika, tomato purée, and salt and pepper to taste. Stir well. Sprinkle the flour on top and stir it in. Add the stock and stir it in well. Add the browned meat to the pot, stir well, cover, and cook for 45 minutes to 1 hour, or until the meat is tender.

Roast Pork Shoulder

6 SERVINGS

1 5-pound pork shoulder with
   skin
Salt
Freshly ground black pepper

1 large onion, peeled and
   chopped
1 teaspoon caraway seeds
1 large can beer

1. Preheat the oven to 375 degrees.

2. Score the pork skin diagonally about ½ inch deep. Sprinkle the meat liberally with salt and pepper. Put the meat, skin side down, in a roasting pan. Sprinkle the chopped onion in the bottom of the pan around the meat. Sprinkle the caraway seeds over the onions. Pour about ½ inch of hot water into the roasting pan. Roast for 1 hour.

3. Remove the pork from the pan. Strain the sauce into a bowl and discard the onion bits. Return the pork to the roasting pan, skin side up. Roast for 2 hours, brushing often with the beer. As the roast cooks, deglaze the pan often with the strained sauce.

4. When the roast is finished, remove the skin and cut into pieces. Slice the meat and put two pieces of skin on each serving. Serve the meat with the sauce from the roasting pan.

Glazed Baked Ham

6 TO 8 SERVINGS

1 4- to 5-pound canned or cured
  ham
Whole cloves

2 tablespoons Dijon mustard
3 tablespoons brown sugar
2 tablespoons orange juice

1. Preheat the oven to 350 degrees.

2. Score the top of the ham in a crossing diagonal pattern. Insert 1 clove where the lines meet. Put the ham in a roasting pan.

3. Combine the mustard, brown sugar, and orange juice in a small saucepan. Bring to a boil and reduce the liquid by half, stirring so it does not stick to the pan. Spread the hot glaze over the top of the ham.

4. Bake for 45 minutes to 1 hour, or until the ham is heated through.

Roast Pork with Prunes

6 SERVINGS

1 2- to 3-pound boneless loin of
  pork
Pitted prunes
1 carrot, trimmed, scraped, and
  chopped

1 celery stalk, trimmed and
  chopped
1 onion, peeled and chopped
1 cup Beef or Chicken Stock
  (see recipes pp. 56 and 58)

1. Preheat the oven to 350 degrees.

2. With a sharp knife make a hole lengthwise through the center of the roast. Enlarge the hole with the handle of a wooden spoon. Push in pitted prunes to fill the hole completely. Put the pork into a roasting pan and roast for ½ hour. Add the vegetables to the pan and roast for 20 to 25 minutes longer, adding a little water from time to time to deglaze the pan.

3. Remove the meat from the pan and let it stand for 10 minutes before carving.

4. Put the roasting pan on top of the stove and pour in the stock. Turn the heat to low, and scrape up any browned-on bits in the roasting pan with a wooden spoon. Pour the sauce over the sliced roast and serve immediately.

Pork Robert

6 SERVINGS

1 tablespoon dry English
    mustard
¼ cup dry white wine
6 slices boneless pork loin
    Salt
    Freshly ground black pepper
    Flour for dredging
3 tablespoons vegetable oil
2 tablespoons chopped
    shallots

¼ cup chopped Kosher dill
    pickles
1 cup Chicken Stock (see recipe
    p. 58)
½ cup heavy cream
3 tablespoons butter or
    margarine
1 pound egg noodles, cooked *al
    dente*
2 tablespoons chopped parsley

1. Dissolve the dry mustard in the white wine and set aside.

2. Pound the pork slices lightly with a flat mallet. Sprinkle the pork slices with salt and pepper and dredge them in flour.

3. Heat the oil in a large frying pan and, when it is hot, add the pork and cook quickly on both sides. This should take only a few minutes; do not overcook the pork. Remove the pork slices to a serving plate and keep them warm.

4. Add the shallots to the frying pan and sauté for 1 minute. Then add the pickles and the mustard dissolved in wine. Add the stock to the frying pan and stir with a wooden spoon to incorporate any browned-on bits in the pan. Stir in the heavy cream and reduce the sauce over medium-high heat for 3 to 4 minutes.

5. Melt the butter in a large frying pan. When it is hot, add the drained cooked noodles, tossing them with the butter until they are heated through and coated with butter.

6. Pour the sauce over the pork slices, garnish with the chopped parsley, and serve with the buttered noodles.

Bombay Pork

6 SERVINGS

6 slices boneless pork loin
   Salt
   Freshly ground black pepper
3 tablespoons vegetable oil
   Curry Sauce (see recipe
     p. 215)
6 slices canned pineapple,
   drained

   Hollandaise Sauce (see recipe
     p. 211)
6 fresh or canned figs, drained
6 slices fresh or canned mango,
   drained
½ cup toasted almond slices

    1. Preheat the broiler.

    2. Pound the pork slices lightly with a flat mallet. Sprinkle them with salt and pepper.

    3. Heat the oil in a large frying pan and, when it is hot, add the pork and cook for 2 minutes on each side. Remove the meat to a flame-proof casserole.

    4. Pour the Curry Sauce over the pork. Put one pineapple slice on each piece of pork. Cover the pineapple with Hollandaise Sauce.

    5. Put the casserole under the broiler for a few minutes until the Hollandaise is lightly browned. Put a fig in the center of each pineapple slice and put the mango slices around the edges of the casserole. Sprinkle the toasted almonds over all and serve immediately.

Pork with Mustard Sauce

6 SERVINGS

6 slices boneless pork loin
   Salt
   Freshly ground black pepper
   Flour for dredging
4 tablespoons vegetable oil

½ cup diced onion
½ cup sliced mushrooms
2 tablespoons Dijon mustard
½ cup dry white wine
½ cup heavy cream

    1. Pound the pork slices lightly with a flat mallet. Sprinkle them with salt and pepper and dredge them in the flour.

2. Heat the oil in a large frying pan and, when it is hot, add the pork slices. Cook for 2 minutes on each side. Add the onion and mushrooms to the pan and sauté for 3 minutes. Then add the mustard and mix well.

3. Remove the pork slices to a serving plate and keep them warm.

4. Add the wine to the pan and reduce it by half. Add the heavy cream and reduce the sauce by half again. Pour the sauce over the pork slices and serve immediately.

Hungarian Pork

6 SERVINGS

6 slices boneless pork loin
  Salt
  Freshly ground black pepper
  Flour for dredging
3 tablespoons vegetable oil
¼ cup minced onion

¼ cup diced bacon
¼ cup diced green or red
   peppers
2 teaspoons paprika
½ cup heavy cream

1. Pound the pork slices lightly with a flat mallet. Sprinkle them with salt and pepper and dredge them in the flour.

2. Heat the oil in a large frying pan and, when it is hot, add the pork slices. Cook for 2 minutes on each side. Transfer the pork slices to a serving plate and keep them warm.

3. Add the onion, bacon, and diced pepper to the oil in the pan and sauté for ½ minute, stirring constantly. Add the paprika and stir and cook for a few seconds. (If you cook it longer, the paprika will burn and turn bitter.)

4. Add the heavy cream to the pan and reduce the sauce by half. Pour the sauce over the warm cutlets and serve immediately.

Red Pepper Pork

6 SERVINGS

6 slices boneless pork loin
  Salt
  Freshly ground black pepper
3 tablespoons vegetable oil

2 large red peppers, seeded and
  sliced
½ cup heavy cream

1. Pound the pork slices lightly with a flat mallet. Sprinkle them with salt and pepper.

2. Heat the oil in a large frying pan and, when it is hot, add the pork. Cook for 2 minutes on each side. Transfer the pork slices to a serving plate and keep them warm.

3. Add the sliced red peppers to the pan and sauté for 2 minutes, stirring constantly. Add the cream and cook for 1 minute. Correct the seasonings, if necessary, and pour the sauce over the pork. Serve immediately.

Pork Budapest

6 SERVINGS

 6 slices boneless pork loin
   Salt
   Freshly ground black pepper
   Flour for dredging
 4 tablespoons vegetable oil
12 slices bacon, diced
 2 onions, peeled and chopped
 2 red peppers or pimientos,
   seeded and diced

2 green peppers, seeded and
  diced
¼ pound boiled ham, diced
1 teaspoon paprika
1 cup Demi-Glace (see recipe
  p. 206)
½ cup heavy cream

1. Pound the pork slices lightly with a flat mallet. Sprinkle them with salt and pepper and dredge them in the flour.

2. Heat the oil in a large frying pan and, when it is hot, add the pork. Cook for 2 minutes on each side. Transfer the pork slices to a plate and keep them warm.

3. Add the bacon to the pan and cook, stirring for 2 minutes. Add the onions, red and green peppers, and ham and sauté for 3 minutes. Sprinkle the paprika over the vegetable mixture and mix it in well. Return the meat to the pan. Pour in the Demi-Glace and cream and cook for 2 minutes, stirring to combine all the ingredients. Serve immediately.

Larded Veal Roast

6 SERVINGS

2 carrots, julienned
2 celery stalks, julienned
1 to 2 cloves garlic, peeled and
    slivered
1 3- to 4-pound shoulder or neck
    of veal

Salt
Freshly ground black pepper
4 tablespoons vegetable oil
½ cup chopped parsley

1. Use a larding needle to insert the carrots, celery, and garlic into the meat. Be sure that the needle is following the direction of the grain of the meat. Season the meat with salt and pepper.

2. Preheat the oven to 375 degrees.

3. Heat the oil in a roasting pan on top of the stove and brown the meat on all sides. Transfer the pan to the oven and roast the meat for 1½ to 2 hours, or until tender. Let the meat rest for 10 minutes before slicing across the grain. Put the slices on a bed of Vichy Carrots (see recipe p. 171) and sprinkle with parsley. Serve immediately.

Osso Bucco

2 whole veal shanks, cut into 1½-inch-thick slices
Salt
Freshly ground black pepper
3 tablespoons vegetable oil
1 onion, peeled and chopped
1 carrot, trimmed, scraped, and chopped
1 leek (white part only), washed well and chopped

2 cloves garlic, peeled and crushed
1 bay leaf
Pinch of dried thyme
1 cup water
2 tomatoes, cored, peeled, seeded, and chopped
3 or 4 tablespoons tomato purée
½ cup dry white wine
2 cups Veal or Chicken Stock (see recipes pp. 57 and 58)

1. Sprinkle the pieces of veal shank with salt and pepper.

2. Heat the oil in a large frying pan and, when it is hot, add the veal and sauté until brown on all sides. Transfer the veal to a baking pan.

3. Preheat the oven to 375 degrees.

4. Add the onion, carrot, celery, leek, and garlic to the frying pan and sauté for 5 minutes. Add the bay leaf, thyme, and water to the pan and stir with a wooden spoon to incorporate any browned-on bits in the pan. Pour the vegetables and sauce over the veal in the baking pan.

5. Bake for 1 hour. Add the tomatoes and tomato purée to the veal and mix in well. Bake for 30 minutes longer, or until the veal is tender. Add more water to the pan, if necessary, to keep the meat from sticking.

6. Add the wine and cook the veal over low heat, stirring with a wooden spoon to pick up any browned-on bits in the pan. Add the stock and cook for 15 to 20 minutes longer. Remove the veal shanks to a serving platter. Strain the sauce over the veal and serve with Risotto Parmesan (see recipe p. 157).

Veal Scallops with Mushrooms

6 SERVINGS

1 pound mushrooms, sliced thin
½ cup water
¼ cup dry white wine
  Salt
  Freshly ground black pepper

6 2-ounce veal scallops
  Flour for dredging
2 tablespoons butter or
  margarine
3 tablespoons chopped parsley

1. Put the mushrooms, ¼ cup of water, and the wine in a saucepan. Season with salt and pepper to taste and cook until the mushrooms are tender.

2. Pound the veal scallops lightly with a flat mallet. Sprinkle them with salt and pepper and dredge them lightly in the flour.

3. Melt the butter in a frying pan, add the remaining water and the veal scallops. Cover the pan and poach the veal until tender, about 15 minutes. Remove the veal to a serving plate and keep warm. Reserve the poaching liquid.

4. Remove the mushrooms from their cooking liquid with a slotted spoon and arrange them around the veal. Reserve the poaching liquid.

5. Pour the mushroom poaching liquid into the veal poaching liquid, bring to a boil, and cook until reduced by half. Add the chopped parsley to the sauce, pour over the veal, and serve immediately.

Veal Orloff

6 SERVINGS

6 slices boneless veal loin
  Salt
  Freshly ground black
    pepper
  Flour for dredging
3 tablespoons butter, margarine,
    or oil

6 slices truffles or sautéed
    mushrooms
1 recipe Soubise Sauce (see
    recipe p. 210)
1 recipe Béchamel Sauce (see
    recipe p. 209)
2 tablespoons chopped parsley

1. Pound the veal lightly with a flat mallet. Sprinkle it with salt and pepper and dredge it in the flour.

2. Melt the butter in a frying pan. Add the veal slices and sauté for 2 minutes on each side. Line the veal up in the center of a serving plate. Top each slice of veal with a slice of truffle.

3. Combine the Soubise and Béchamel sauces and spoon the mixture over the veal and truffles. Sprinkle with parsley and serve at once.

Wiener Schnitzel

6 SERVINGS

6 slices boneless veal loin
  Salt
  Freshly ground black pepper
  Flour for dredging
2 eggs, beaten
  Bread crumbs for coating

6 tablespoons butter or
    margarine
6 anchovy fillets
6 thin lemon slices
12 capers

1. Pound the veal slices with a flat mallet. Sprinkle them with salt and pepper and dredge them in the flour. Dip the veal slices in the beaten eggs and then in the bread crumbs. Press the bread crumbs on with the palm of your hand. Put the breaded veal slices on a flat plate,

making sure they do not touch. Separate the layers with wax paper. Refrigerate for 10 minutes before cooking.

2. Melt the butter in a frying pan and add the breaded veal, making sure the veal slices do not touch each other. Sauté for 8 to 10 minutes, turning once, or until the veal is golden brown on both sides. Garnish each piece with an anchovy fillet, a lemon slice, and 2 capers, and serve at once.

Veal Involtini alla Morandi

6 SERVINGS

6 veal scallops
  Salt
  Freshly ground black pepper
6 slices prosciutto or boiled ham
6 slices mozzarella or Swiss
  cheese
6 large fresh basil leaves

4 tablespoons vegetable or olive
  oil, or a combination of
  both
1 cup dry red wine
1 cup Chicken or Veal Stock
  (see recipes pp. 58 and 57)
½ cup tomato purée

1. Pound the veal scallops lightly with a flat mallet. Sprinkle with salt and pepper. Put a slice of prosciutto and a slice of cheese on top of each scallop. Top with a basil leaf and roll up and close with a toothpick.

2. Heat the oil in a saucepan large enough to hold the veal rolls in one layer. When hot, add the veal rolls and sauté on all sides for a few minutes. Add the red wine, stock, and tomato purée to the pan and mix well. Bring to a boil, cover, lower the heat, and simmer for 35 minutes, or until the veal is tender. Remove the toothpicks before serving. This is very nice served with pasta.

Veal Birds

6 SERVINGS

6 veal scallops
  Salt
  Freshly ground black pepper
6 thin slices boiled ham
6 hard-cooked eggs
  Flour for dredging

4 tablespoons butter or
    margarine
½ cup dry Marsala
½ cup Veal or Chicken Stock
    (see recipes pp. 57 and 58)

1. Pound the veal scallops lightly with a flat mallet. Season them with salt and pepper. Put a piece of ham on each piece of veal. Put a hard-cooked egg in the center and roll up the veal and secure closed with a toothpick. Dredge the veal rolls in flour.

2. Preheat the oven to 350 degrees.

3. Melt the butter in a large frying pan. When hot, add the veal rolls and sauté them, turning until they are browned on all sides. Pour in the wine and stock and bake for 30 minutes, or until the veal is tender.

4. To serve, remove the toothpicks (they are very hard to chew) and slice each veal roll in half. Put the rolls on a bed of fresh spinach and pour some of the sauce over them. Serve the rest of the sauce separately. This dish goes very well with Farina Dumplings (see recipe p. 162).

Assiette Diplomat

6 SERVINGS

4 tablespoons vegetable oil
1½ pounds boneless veal, cut
    into slivers
  Salt
  Freshly ground black pepper
¾ cup chopped onion

1½ cups chopped mushrooms
1½ cups diced Swiss cheese
1½ cups dry white wine
¾ cup heavy cream
  Lemon juice
½ cup chopped parsley

1. Heat the oil in a frying pan. When it is hot, add the veal slivers and sauté for 2 minutes, stirring constantly. Season with salt and pepper to taste. Add the chopped onion and mushrooms and sauté for 5 minutes longer, stirring occasionally. Add the diced cheese and stir well.

2. Add the wine and cream and stir with a wooden spoon to incorporate any browned-on bits from the pan into the sauce. Add lemon juice to taste and correct the seasonings, if necessary. Serve garnished with parsley.

Veal Stew with Vegetables

6 SERVINGS

4 tablespoons vegetable oil
1½ pounds shoulder or neck
    veal, cubed
1 large onion, peeled and sliced
1 bay leaf
    Salt
    Freshly ground black pepper

2 cups Chicken Stock (see
    recipe p. 58)
1 cup scraped and diced carrots
1½ cups peeled and diced
    potatoes (optional)
1 cup cauliflower flowerets

1. Heat the oil in a large saucepan. When it is hot, add the veal cubes and sauté until they are brown. Add the onion, bay leaf, salt and pepper to taste, and the stock. Stir well. Simmer, covered, for ½ hour, or until the veal is just tender, stirring occasionally.

2. Add the carrots, potatoes, and cauliflower and cook for 10 to 15 minutes, or until the vegetables are tender. Correct the seasonings, if necessary, and serve right away.

Veal Pojarski

6 SERVINGS

6 slices trimmed white bread
3 tablespoons butter or
    margarine
1 small onion, peeled and
    minced
1 pound ground veal
2 eggs

Salt
Freshly ground black pepper
Pinch of ground nutmeg
6 pieces elbow macaroni
4 tablespoons vegetable oil
    Brown Cream Sauce (see
        following recipe)

1. Soak the bread in water until soft. Squeeze dry and set aside.

2. Melt the butter in a small frying pan. Add the onion and sauté for 5 minutes, stirring occasionally.

3. Mix the meat, bread, onions, eggs, salt and pepper to taste, and nutmeg together. Divide the mixture into six equal parts. Shape each part to resemble a loin pork chop. Press a piece of uncooked macaroni on the inside edge where the bone should be.

4. Preheat the oven to 400 degrees.

5. Heat the oil in a frying pan. When it is hot, add the "chops" and brown on both sides. Transfer the chops to a baking dish as they brown. (Save the drippings in the frying pan. You will need them to make the Brown Cream Sauce.)

6. Bake for 30 minutes, or until cooked through. Serve with Brown Cream Sauce on the side.

Brown Cream Sauce

1 small onion, peeled and
    chopped
½ cup dry white wine
1 cup Veal or Chicken Stock
    (see recipes pp. 57 and 58)

Salt
Freshly ground black pepper
Juice of ½ lemon
½ cup heavy cream
2 tablespoons chopped parsley

Sauté the chopped onion until soft in the drippings in the frying pan in which you browned the veal chops. Add the wine and stir with a wooden spoon to scrape up any browned-on bits in the pan. Add the stock, salt and pepper to taste, and the lemon juice. Cook for 2 minutes. Add the cream and the parsley and cook for a minute, but do not boil.

NOTE: If the sauce is too thin, you can thicken it by adding a little *beurre manié*, which is just a mixture of butter and flour. Cream together 1 teaspoon of softened butter and 1 teaspoon of flour. Stir the mixture into the sauce a little bit at a time, until the sauce is the consistency you want.

Irish Stew

6 SERVINGS

2 tablespoons vegetable oil
2 onions, peeled and sliced
2 cloves garlic, peeled and
  minced
2 pounds boneless lamb, cubed
1 bay leaf
  Salt

Freshly ground black pepper
1 small head of cabbage, cored
  and cut into ½-inch dice
2 small carrots, trimmed,
  scraped, and sliced
4 potatoes, peeled and diced
2 tablespoons chopped parsley

1. Heat the oil in a large heavy pot. Add the sliced onions and the garlic and sauté for 7 to 8 minutes. Add the lamb and sauté for 5 minutes more, stirring occasionally. Add the bay leaf and enough water to cover the meat and vegetables by 2 inches. Season with salt and pepper to taste and bring to a boil. Lower the heat, cover, and simmer for 45 minutes.

2. Add the cabbage, carrots, and potatoes and cook for 20 minutes, or until the vegetables and meat are tender. Correct the seasonings, if necessary. Sprinkle with parsley and serve hot.

NOTE: This dish is usually served with dumplings, but I prefer to add potatoes to the stew.

Stuffed Breast of Lamb

6 SERVINGS

1 3-pound breast of lamb
1 tablespoon butter or
   margarine
½ cup chopped onion
½ cup chopped celery
1 cup boiling milk
   Pinch of ground nutmeg
   Salt
   Freshly ground black pepper
2 eggs

2 tablespoons chopped parsley
3 stale seedless rolls, sliced
¼ cup oil
1 onion, peeled and chopped
1 cup chopped carrots
1 cup chopped celery
2 cloves garlic, peeled
2 cups water
2 tablespoons tomato purée

1. Cut a pocket in the breast for the stuffing by cutting away the meat of the breast as close to the bones as possible. Do not cut all the way through or the stuffing will seep out.

2. Melt the butter in a large frying pan and add the onion and celery. Sauté for 5 to 10 minutes, or until the onion is soft. Remove from the heat and pour in the boiling milk. Cover and let sit for 5 minutes. Add the nutmeg and salt and pepper to taste. Mix in the eggs, parsley, and sliced rolls until you have a sticky paste. Let cool.

3. Sprinkle the lamb inside and out with salt and pepper. Put the stuffing in the prepared pocket and close the pocket securely with toothpicks.

4. Preheat the oven to 350 degrees.

5. Heat the oil in a roasting pan large enough to hold the lamb comfortably. Brown the meat on both sides, turning carefully so the stuffing does not come out. Add the onion, carrots, celery, and garlic to the roasting pan. Roast for 1 hour.

6. Remove the pan from the oven and stir the water and tomato purée into the pan drippings and vegetables. Return the roast to the oven and bake for 1 to 1½ hours longer, or until the meat is tender, stirring the pan drippings and basting the meat frequently with the pan drippings.

7. Remove the roast and vegetables to a serving platter and let them rest while you finish the sauce.

8. Degrease the pan drippings. Put the roasting pan over medium-high heat and reduce the pan drippings by half. Strain the sauce over the meat and serve.

Broiled Lamb Chops

6 SERVINGS

6 double loin lamb chops
  Salt
  Freshly ground black pepper
4 tablespoons chopped parsley

4 tablespoons bread crumbs
4 tablespoons Dijon mustard
2 cloves garlic, peeled and
  minced

1. Preheat the broiler.

2. Sprinkle the chops on both sides with salt and pepper. Broil the chops 5 inches from the flame for 8 minutes.

3. While the chops are broiling on one side, mix the parsley, bread crumbs, mustard, and garlic together in a small bowl.

4. Turn the chops over and spread the seasoning mixture in equal portions over the tops of the chops. Broil for 5 minutes, until golden brown. The chops should be done to medium.

Roast Leg of Lamb

6 TO 8 SERVINGS

1 5- to 7-pound leg of lamb
4 to 5 cloves garlic, peeled
  Salt

  Freshly ground black pepper
  Crushed dried rosemary
¼ cup vegetable oil

1. Make small holes in the flesh of the lamb with a paring knife. Insert a clove of garlic in each hole. (Don't bunch the holes together, but spread them out over the surface of the meat.) Sprinkle the meat liberally with salt, pepper, and rosemary. Rub the spices into the meat with your fingers.

2. Preheat the oven to 375 degrees.

3. Heat the oil in a roasting pan large enough to hold the leg of lamb. When the oil is hot, add the lamb and brown it all over. Before you put the lamb in the oven, be sure to turn it right side up (that's the rounded side).

4. Roast for 20 to 25 minutes per pound for medium. Let the lamb sit a few minutes before you carve it.

Lamb Curry

6 SERVINGS

8 tablespoons vegetable oil
2 large onions, peeled and chopped
2 apples, peeled, cored, and chopped
1 cup all-purpose flour
1 tablespoon curry powder

4 cups Chicken or Veal Stock, heated (see recipes pp. 58 and 57)
Salt
Freshly ground black pepper
2½ to 3 pounds boneless lamb, cut into ½-inch cubes
½ cup heavy cream

1. Heat 4 tablespoons of oil in a large saucepan. Add the onions and apples and sauté until they are light brown. Stir occasionally so they do not stick. Add the flour and stir it in so that it coats the onions and apples. Add the curry powder, mix well, and cook for 1 minute. Gradually add the hot stock, stirring constantly. Season with salt and pepper to taste. Bring the sauce to a boil, lower the heat, and let it simmer while you prepare the meat.

2. Preheat the oven to 350 degrees.

3. Heat the remaining 4 tablespoons of oil in a large frying pan. Add the lamb cubes and sauté them until they are browned on all sides.

4. Put the browned lamb cubes in a large casserole and pour in the simmering curry sauce. Bake for 1 to 1½ hours, or until the meat is tender.

5. Remove the meat from the sauce and put it in a bowl. Strain the sauce into a clean saucepan and add the cream. Return the meat to the sauce and correct the seasonings, if necessary. Heat for just 1 minute. Serve hot, with rice and chutney, if desired.

Shish Kebab

6 TO 8 SERVINGS

1 pound boned lamb
1 pound boned veal
1 pound boned pork
1 large green pepper
2 onions, peeled and cut into
    quarters
2 cloves garlic, peeled and
    crushed

1 teaspoon dried oregano
1 bay leaf
Salt
Freshly ground black pepper
½ cup vegetable oil
Juice of 2 lemons

1. Cut all the meat into evenly sized and shaped cubes. Pound the cubes with a flat mallet to tenderize them.

2. Cut the pepper into pieces about the same size as the pieces of onion.

3. Thread the meats on skewers, alternating with the onion and green pepper. Lay the skewers flat in a large glass or ceramic dish.

4. Combine the garlic, oregano, bay leaf, salt and pepper to taste, oil, and lemon juice in a small bowl. Mix well and pour over the prepared kebabs. Turn the kebabs in the marinade to coat them evenly. Cover tightly with foil and refrigerate for several hours or overnight. Turn the kebabs every few hours as they are marinating.

5. To cook, drain the kebabs and broil them about 4 inches from the heat for 12 to 15 minutes, turning every few minutes so they cook evenly. The kebabs can also be grilled over hot coals or sautéed in a little hot oil in a frying pan. Serve with Curried Rice (see recipe p. 159).

Lamb and Bean Stew

6 SERVINGS

4 tablespoons vegetable oil
2½ pounds boneless lamb
    shoulder, cut into cubes
    Salt
    Freshly ground black pepper
2 onions, peeled and sliced
2 cloves garlic, peeled and
    minced

2 cups Chicken Stock (see
    recipe p. 58)
2 potatoes, peeled and sliced
½ pound string beans, trimmed
    and washed

1. Heat the oil in a large heavy pot. Add the lamb and sauté, stirring occasionally, until the cubes are browned on all sides. Season with salt and pepper to taste. Add the onions, garlic, and stock and bring to a boil. Cover, lower the heat, and simmer for 1 hour, or until the meat is just barely tender.

2. Add the potatoes and string beans and cook for 20 minutes, or until the vegetables are very tender. Correct the seasonings, if necessary, and serve hot.

NOTE: If the stew dries out too much while you are cooking it, add more stock or water.

Swabian Lamb Stew

6 SERVINGS

4 tablespoons oil
1 clove garlic, peeled and
    minced
3 pounds boneless lamb, such
    as shoulder, neck, or
    breast, cut in ½-inch cubes
4 tablespoons all-purpose flour
    Salt

    Freshly ground black pepper
3 cups water
1½ cups dry white wine
1 bay leaf
3 small onions, peeled, each
    studded with 2 cloves
1 lemon, cut in half

Heat the oil in a large saucepan. Add the garlic and sauté for 2 minutes. Add the lamb and sauté until lightly browned on all sides. Sprinkle with the flour and salt and pepper to taste. Mix well. Add the water and wine and mix in well. Add the bay leaf, onions, and lemon halves and bring to a boil. Cover, lower the heat, and simmer for 1 hour, or until the meat is tender. Remove the bay leaf, onions, and lemons. Correct the seasonings, if necessary. Serve with rice or Spätzle (see recipe p. 162).

6

Poultry

Stuffed Chicken Rolls on a Bed of Stir-Fried Vegetables and
Roast Turkey with Stuffing Loaf.

Most of us find ourselves eating more chicken these days than
we used to. After all, it is the least expensive meat around, and it
is low in calories and cholesterol, pound for pound. So here are
some nice recipes for chicken that are easy to do, and there are
enough of them so people won't say, "What? Chicken again?"

I have also included some recipes for Cornish hens, turkey,
duck, and goose, which make a good change when you really get
tired of chicken.

Barbecued Chicken

6 TO 8 SERVINGS

2 chickens
　Grated peel of 1 orange
　Grated peel of 1 lemon
¼ cup vinegar
¼ cup vegetable oil
½ cup ketchup

½ cup honey
¼ cup blackstrap molasses
¼ cup chopped onion
　Juice of 1 orange
　Juice of 1 lemon
　Pinch of salt

1. Preheat the oven to 375 degrees.

2. Cut the chickens through the back to remove the backbones and breastbones (see p. 8), but leave the chickens attached at the breast area. Flatten the chickens well. Put them skin side up, on a baking sheet, and roast for 25 minutes.

3. While the chickens are cooking, make the barbecue sauce by combining the grated orange and lemon peels, vinegar, oil, ketchup, honey, molasses, onion, orange and lemon juices, and the salt in a saucepan. Bring to a boil and cook for 15 to 20 minutes, or until the sauce is reduced by half. (The color will change from light to dark red as the sauce cooks.)

4. When the chickens have cooked for 25 minutes, brush them on all sides with the barbecue sauce. Cook, brushing several times more, until the chickens are tender. Serve with additional sauce, if you want.

NOTE: If you like a sweeter sauce, you can add a little brown sugar to the barbecue sauce before you begin to boil it. The chickens can also be cooked on a barbecue grill. Just bake them in the oven for 25 minutes and then transfer them to the grill, brush them with the sauce, and cook them until they are done.

Poulet Celestine

6 to 8 SERVINGS

6 tablespoons butter or
  margarine
2 2½- to 3-pound chickens, cut
  up (see p. 8)
1 pound mushrooms, sliced
2 tomatoes, cored, peeled,
  seeded, and diced
2 cups dry white wine
¾ cup Cognac or brandy

1 cup Chicken Stock (see recipe
  p. 58)
⅛ teaspoon cayenne pepper
  Salt
  Freshly ground black pepper
2 cloves garlic, peeled and
  minced
4 tablespoons chopped parsley

1. Melt the butter in a large frying pan. Add the chicken and sauté over high heat until golden brown. Be sure to turn the chicken often while you are sautéing it.

2. Add the mushrooms and tomatoes and cook for 5 minutes.

3. Add the wine, Cognac, stock, cayenne, and salt and pepper to taste. Mix in well, cover, and cook for 35 minutes, or until the chicken is done. Remove the chicken and keep it warm on a serving platter.

4. Skim the grease from the top of the sauce. Add the garlic and parsley to the sauce and boil the sauce over high heat for a few minutes to reduce it a little. Pour the sauce over the chicken and serve.

Coq au Vin

6 to 8 SERVINGS

2 chickens, cut into quarters
  Salt
  Freshly ground black pepper
8 tablespoons butter or
  margarine
2 onions, peeled and chopped

4 carrots, turned (see p. 7)
20 mushroom caps, cut in half
4 tablespoons all-purpose flour
2 cups dry white wine
2 cups Chicken Stock (see
  recipe p. 58)

1. Sprinkle the chicken with salt and pepper.

2. Melt the butter in a large frying pan and sauté the chicken until it is lightly browned. Transfer the chicken pieces to an ovenproof casserole as they brown.

3. Preheat the oven to 350 degrees.

4. Add the onions, carrots, and mushrooms to the frying pan and sauté them for 5 minutes. Sprinkle the flour over the vegetables and stir it in. Slowly add the wine, stirring constantly. Stir in the stock and season the sauce with salt and pepper to taste. Bring the sauce just to the boiling point and pour it over the chicken in the casserole. Cover the casserole and bake for 45 minutes to 1 hour, or until the chicken is tender. Serve with Noodles with Shallot Butter (see recipe p. 148).

Tarragon Chicken

6 SERVINGS

3 whole chicken breasts, boned
    and skinned (see p. 12)
    Salt
    Freshly ground black pepper
5 tablespoons butter, margarine,
    or oil
3 tablespoons chopped shallots

¾ cup dry white wine
¾ cup heavy cream
3 tablespoons chopped fresh
    tarragon
    Beurre manié, if needed (see
    note p. 95)

1. Cut the chicken breasts in half and sprinkle them on both sides with salt and pepper.

2. Melt the butter in a large frying pan and sauté the chicken breasts until they are golden brown and cooked through. Turn them often as you are sautéing them so that they cook evenly. Remove the chicken breasts to a serving platter and keep them warm.

3. Add the shallots to the frying pan and sauté for 2 minutes, stirring constantly. Pour in the white wine and stir it around with a wooden spoon to scrape up any browned-on bits in the frying pan. Add the cream and the tarragon and stir to blend. If the sauce is too thin, add the *beurre manié*. Pour the sauce over the chicken and serve immediately.

Suprême Normande

6 SERVINGS

6 tablespoons butter or
  margarine
4 apples, peeled, cored, and
  sliced
3 whole chicken breasts, boned
  and skinned (see p. 12)
  Salt

Freshly ground black pepper
Flour for dredging
½ cup Calvados or applejack
¼ cup Chicken Stock (see recipe
  p. 58)
½ cup heavy cream
3 tablespoons chopped parsley

1. Melt 2 tablespoons of butter in a small frying pan. Add 1 of the sliced apples and sauté until it is barely tender. Remove the apple slices from the pan and set them aside to be used as garnish.

2. Split the chicken breasts in half and sprinkle them with salt and pepper and dredge them in the flour.

3. Melt the remaining butter in a large frying pan and add the chicken breasts in one layer. (Do not crowd them or they will not brown properly. If you have to, cook them in 2 batches, adding more butter, if necessary.) Sauté the breasts until browned on both sides. Add the remaining apples to the pan and cook for 5 to 10 minutes, or until the chicken is tender. Remove the chicken and keep it warm.

4. Add the Calvados and stock to the frying pan. Stir with a wooden spoon to scrape up any browned-on bits in the pan. Turn the heat to medium-high and reduce the sauce a little. Stir the cream into the pan, correct seasonings, if necessary, and pour the hot sauce over the chicken. Garnish the dish with the reserved sautéed apple slices and the chopped parsley and serve immediately.

Stuffed Chicken Rolls

6 SERVINGS

3 whole chicken breasts
 Salt
 Freshly ground black pepper
 Spinach-Cheese Stuffing (see
   recipe below)
 Spinach Stuffing (see receipe
   below)

Flour for dredging
6 tablespoons butter, margarine,
   or oil
 Stir-Fried Vegetables (see
   recipe p. 184)

1. Skin and bone the chicken breasts and butterfly them (see pp. 12 and Note below). Sprinkle the chicken with salt and pepper.

2. Prepare either one of the stuffings and spread some of it in the center of each breast. Roll the breasts up and close them with tooth-picks or string. Dredge the chicken rolls in flour.

3. Preheat the oven to 375 degrees. Put 2 tablespoons of butter in a roasting pan large enough to hold the chicken rolls and put the pan in the oven so the butter melts while you are sautéing the chicken rolls.

4. Melt the remaining butter in a frying pan and add the chicken rolls. Sauté them in the butter until they are brown on all sides. Transfer the chicken rolls to the roasting pan and bake them for 15 minutes, or until they are just tender. Don't forget to remove the toothpicks or string. They will make the rolls hard to chew.) Serve over a bed of Stir-Fried Vegetables.

NOTE: To butterfly chicken breasts, lay them flat on a cutting board, skin side up. Hold your knife horizontal to the cutting board and cut almost through each chicken breast, from one side to the other. If you do this properly, the breast will look like the open pages of a book. Be careful not to split the breast completely. Pound the breasts lightly, especially in the center, to even them out.

Spinach-Cheese Stuffing

1 10-ounce package fresh
   spinach
½ cup ricotta cheese
2 tablespoons butter or
   margarine, softened

2 tablespoons grated Parmesan
   cheese
Pinch of ground nutmeg
Salt
Freshly ground black pepper

1. Pick over the spinach to remove the stems and any bruised leaves. Wash it well and drain it. Blanch the spinach in boiling water, refresh it under cold running water, and squeeze it dry. Chop well.

2. Combine the spinach with the ricotta, butter, Parmesan, nutmeg, and salt and pepper to taste. Mix well.

Spinach Stuffing

2 10-ounce packages fresh
   spinach
2 tablespoons butter or
   margarine
1 onion, peeled and minced
2 anchovy fillets

Pinch of ground nutmeg
Salt
Freshly ground black pepper
2 tablespoons grated Parmesan
   cheese (optional)

1. Pick over the spinach to remove the stems and any bruised leaves. Wash it well and drain it. Blanch the spinach in boiling water, refresh it under cold running water, and squeeze it dry. Chop well.

2. Melt the butter in a frying pan and add the onion. Sauté until soft. Mash the anchovies and add them to the onion. Add the spinach, nutmeg, and salt and pepper to taste. Sauté for 3 to 4 minutes. Add the cheese, if desired. Cool the stuffing before using.

Chicken Breasts Florentine

6 SERVINGS

2 10-ounce packages fresh spinach
6 pieces boneless chicken breast (see p. 12)
Flour for dredging
¾ cup water
1¼ cups dry white wine
6 anchovy fillets (optional)
Pinch of ground nutmeg
Salt
Freshly ground black pepper
12 tomato wedges
6 lemon wedges

1. Pick over the spinach to remove the stems and any bruised leaves. Wash it well and drain it. Blanch the spinach in boiling water, refresh it under cold running water, and squeeze it dry. Chop the spinach coarsely.

2. Pound the chicken breasts lightly to make them even. Dredge them in the flour.

3. Bring the water and wine to a boil in a large frying pan. Put the chicken breasts into the boiling liquid, cover, and poach for 5 minutes.

4. While the chicken is poaching, put the anchovies and the chopped spinach into a nonstick frying pan. Heat slowly so they do not burn. Season with the nutmeg and salt and pepper to taste. Sauté for a few minutes to warm completely.

5. Put equal portions of the spinach on serving plates and top each with a chicken breast. Pour some of the poaching liquid over the chicken and spinach and garnish the dishes with tomato wedges and lemon wedges. Serve immediately.

Curried Chicken

6 SERVINGS

6 pieces boneless chicken breast,
   skinned (see p. 12)
Salt
Freshly ground black pepper
3 tablespoons butter, margarine,
   or oil
1 red pepper, seeded and diced
½ green pepper, seeded and
   diced

1 onion, peeled and chopped
1 small can diced pineapple,
   drained
1 tablespoon curry powder
½ cup dry white wine
2 tablespoons chopped parsley
½ cup toasted almond slices

1. Cut the chicken into small cubes. Season the cubes with salt and pepper.

2. Melt the butter in a frying pan and add the cubed chicken. Sauté, tossing constantly, for 3 to 4 minutes. Remove the chicken with a slotted spoon and put it in a bowl.

3. Add the peppers, onion, and pineapple to the frying pan and cook for 3 minutes. Sprinkle the curry powder over the vegetables and stir it in quickly. Immediately add the wine and stir it in well. Return the chicken to the pan to heat through. Garnish with chopped parsley and almonds. Serve with Saffron Rice (see recipe p. 158) and Sautéed Apple Slices (see recipe p. 203).

Chicken Cordon Bleu

6 SERVINGS

6 whole chicken breasts, with
   breastbone removed (see
   p. 12)
6 slices boiled ham
6 slices Swiss cheese

Flour for dredging
2 eggs
Bread crumbs for coating
6 tablespoons butter or
   margarine

1. Skin the chicken breasts and pound them lightly.

2. Spread the breasts out, skin side down, and lay a slice of ham on each one. Top the ham with a slice of cheese. Fold the breasts over and hold closed with a toothpick or two.

3. Put a good amount of flour on a piece of wax paper. Beat the eggs in a flat soup plate. Put a good amount of bread crumbs on a piece of wax paper.

4. Dredge each chicken breast in the flour, dip it into the eggs, and then coat with the bread crumbs (see p. 14). As the chicken breasts are coated, lay them on a flat plate, making sure they do not touch. Separate the layers with wax paper. Refrigerate for 10 minutes.

5. Melt the butter in a large frying pan, add the chicken breasts, and sauté them for 5 to 6 minutes on each side, or until golden brown. (You can also melt the butter in a roasting pan and bake the chicken in a 400-degree oven for 15 minutes, or until it is cooked.) Remove the toothpicks carefully and serve immediately.

Chicken Pompadour

6 SERVINGS

6 pieces boneless chicken breast, skinned (see p. 12)
Salt
Freshly ground black pepper
2 eggs

Flour for dredging
2 cups chopped, blanched almonds
6 tablespoons butter or margarine

1. Pound the chicken breasts lightly to even them. Season them with salt and pepper.

2. Beat the eggs in a flat soup plate. Put a good amount of flour on a piece of wax paper. Put the almonds on a piece of wax paper.

3. Dredge each chicken breast in the flour, dip it into the eggs, and then coat it with the almonds. Press with the palm of your hand so that the almonds will stick to the chicken.

4. Melt the butter in a large frying pan and sauté the chicken breasts for 4 to 5 minutes on each side, or until cooked through and golden brown. Serve immediately.

Chicken Breasts with Beurre Blanc Sauce

6 SERVINGS

6 pieces boneless chicken breast, skinned (see p. 12)
Salt
Freshly ground black pepper
6 tablespoons butter or margarine

⅓ cup finely minced onion
¾ cup dry white wine
¾ cup heavy cream
3 tablespoons chopped parsley

1. Sprinkle the chicken breasts with salt and pepper.

2. Melt the butter in a frying pan large enough to hold the chicken in one layer. Add the chicken breasts and sauté for 5 minutes on each side. (Do not let the butter burn.) Remove the chicken breasts to a serving plate and keep them warm.

3. Add the onion to the frying pan and sauté for 2 minutes, stirring occasionally. Add the wine, stir, and reduce by half. Add the cream and cook, stirring constantly for 2 minutes. Add the parsley and cook for 1 minute. Correct the seasonings, if necessary. Pour the sauce over the chicken and serve immediately.

Chicken Legs Stuffed with Sauerkraut

6 SERVINGS

6 whole chicken legs
Salt
Freshly ground black pepper
1 10-ounce can sauerkraut
2 small red peppers, seeded and diced
2 small green peppers, seeded and diced

Flour for dredging
5 tablespoons vegetable oil
1½ tablespoons paprika
1½ cups Chicken Stock (see recipe p. 58)

1. Bone the legs, making sure that you do not cut through the meat (see p. 10). Spread the meat out and pound it to even it out. Sprinkle with salt and pepper.

2. Blanch the sauerkraut in boiling water, rinse, and drain well, squeezing out all the moisture. Mix the diced peppers with the sauerkraut and season with salt and pepper to taste.

3. Stuff each chicken leg with some of the sauerkraut mixture. Roll the meat closed and either tie it with string or fasten it with toothpicks. Dredge the rolls in the flour.

4. Preheat the oven to 375 degrees.

5. Heat the oil in an ovenproof pan and brown the rolls on all sides. Stir in the paprika and then the stock.

6. Bake for 45 minutes, or until the meat is tender. Remove the chicken and keep it warm. (Don't forget to remove the string or toothpicks.) Reduce the sauce by half over medium-high heat, stirring occasionally. Correct the seasonings, if necessary, and pour the sauce over the chicken. Serve with noodles, rice, or potatoes.

Grenadines of Chicken

6 SERVINGS

6 chicken legs	4 tablespoons vegetable oil
Salt	2 eggs
Freshly ground black pepper	1 tablespoon water
Flour for dredging	

1. Skin and bone the chicken legs (see p. 10). Cut each piece in two and pound flat with a mallet. Season with salt and pepper and dredge in the flour.

2. Preheat the oven to 375 degrees.

3. Heat the oil in a frying pan.

4. Beat the eggs and water together in a flat soup plate. When the oil is hot, dip the floured chicken pieces into the egg mixture and put them into the hot oil. Brown quickly on both sides. Transfer the chicken pieces to a small baking pan as they brown.

5. Bake for 30 minutes, or until cooked through. Serve immediately.

Chicken Quenelles

6 SERVINGS

1 pound boneless chicken breast,
  cut into cubes
5 egg whites
7 slices trimmed white bread,
  soaked in water and
  squeezed dry
1 cup clarified butter (see p. 211)

Salt
Freshly ground black pepper
6 cups hot Chicken Stock (see
  recipe p. 58)
Tarragon Cream Sauce (see
  recipe p. 209)

    1. Put the chicken into the container of a food processor and grind it thoroughly. Add the egg whites and process for a few seconds. Add the bread and then the butter, processing after each addition. Season with salt and pepper to taste.

    2. Form the quenelles by following the directions on p. 17. Drop the quenelles into the hot stock and poach for 5 minutes. Drain and add to the Tarragon Cream Sauce before serving.

Cornish Hens with Vegetables

6 SERVINGS

6 small Cornish hens
  Salt
  Freshly ground black pepper
3 cups chopped onions
2 cups chopped parsley

6 tablespoons butter or
  margarine
2 cups julienned carrots (see p. 5).
1 pound mushrooms, sliced
1 cup dry white wine

    1. Sprinkle the hens inside and out with salt and pepper.

    2. Mix together the onions and 1½ cups chopped parsley. Use the mixture to stuff the hens. Truss the hens.

3. Melt the butter in a frying pan and sauté the hens on all sides for 5 minutes. (This will seal the meat so that it will be juicier.) Do not clean the pan out.

4. Preheat the oven to 350 degrees.

5. Transfer the browned hens to a roasting pan (use two if you have to) and bake them for 35 to 40 minutes.

6. When the hens are almost cooked, heat the frying pan in which you sautéed them and add the carrots, mushrooms, and the remaining parsley. Sauté for 5 minutes and add the wine. Reduce the wine by half and season the vegetables with salt and pepper to taste.

7. Arrange the vegetables on a serving platter. Remove the hens from the oven and cut them in half. Remove the stuffing and put it on top of the vegetables. Arrange the hen halves on top and serve immediately.

Cornish Hens with Cabbage

6 SERVINGS

6 tablespoons butter or margarine
1 large onion, peeled and chopped
2 carrots, trimmed, scraped, and minced
2 apples, peeled, cored, and diced
1 large head green cabbage, cored and shredded
1 cup dry white wine
Juice of 1 lemon
Few juniper berries, crushed
Salt
Freshly ground black pepper
6 small Cornish hens
4 tablespoons vegetable oil
3 tablespoons Cognac
½ cup chopped parsley

1. Melt the butter in a large frying pan and add the onion, carrots, and apples. Sauté for 5 minutes, stirring occasionally. Add the cabbage and cook, stirring, until wilted. Add the white wine, lemon juice, and juniper berries and mix well. Season with salt and pepper to taste. Transfer the mixture to the bottom of a large buttered baking dish.

2. Preheat the oven to 375 degrees.

3. Sprinkle the hens inside and out with salt and pepper. Brush them with some of the oil. Heat the remaining oil in a frying pan and brown the hens on all sides. As they brown, transfer the hens to the baking dish.

4. When the hens have all been browned, pour the Cognac into the frying pan and stir with a wooden spoon to scrape up any browned-on bits in the pan. Pour the sauce over the hens. Roast for 40 minutes, or until nicely brown and cooked. Baste the hens occasionally with the pan juices as they roast. Garnish the dish with the parsley and serve right from the baking dish.

NOTE: You may have to use two baking dishes. Just be sure to divide the cabbage mixture and sauce evenly between the two dishes.

Cornish Hens Derby

6 SERVINGS

Liver and Rice Pilaf (see
　recipe below)
6 Cornish hens
Salt
Freshly ground black pepper
3 tablespoons butter or
　margarine
3 tablespoons vegetable oil
2 carrots, trimmed, scraped,
　and chopped
2 celery stalks, trimmed and
　chopped
1 large onion, peeled and
　chopped
1½ tablespoons tomato paste
　Pinch of dried thyme
¾ cup dry red wine
3 cups Chicken Stock (see
　recipe p. 58)
¾ cup heavy cream

1. Prepare the Liver and Rice Pilaf and let it cool.

2. Sprinkle the hens inside and out with salt and pepper. Stuff with the pilaf and truss.

3. Heat the butter and oil in a large frying pan and brown the hens on all sides. Remove the hens to a platter and keep warm.

4. Add the carrots, celery, and onion to the frying pan and stir well. Add the tomato paste and thyme and stir again. Pour in the wine and stir with a wooden spoon to scrape up any browned-on bits in the pan. Add the stock and season the sauce with salt and pepper to taste. Return the hens to the pan and cook, covered, for 45 minutes, or until they are done. Remove the hens to a serving platter and keep warm.

5. Strain the sauce and degrease it. Add the cream and heat through. Pour the sauce over the hens and serve immediately.

NOTE: If you don't have a frying pan large enough to hold all the hens comfortably, you can cook them in two large frying pans. Just divide the sauce equally *before* you return the hens to the sauce. Bring both pans of sauce to a simmer, add the hens, and continue with the recipe.

Liver and Rice Pilaf

5 tablespoons butter or margarine	Livers from the Cornish hens
3 tablespoons minced onion or shallots	Pinch of cayenne
5 large mushrooms, chopped	Salt
1 cup rice	Freshly ground black pepper
1½ cups Chicken Stock (see recipe p. 58)	3 slices liver pâté, diced
	1 tablespoon chopped truffles (optional)
	2 tablespoons chopped parsley

1. Preheat the oven to 375 degrees.

2. Melt 3 tablespoons of butter in an ovenproof pot. Add the onion and mushrooms and sauté for 5 minutes. Add the rice and stir to coat with the butter. Pour in the stock and bring to a boil on top of the stove. Cover and bake for 18 minutes.

3. Melt the remaining butter in a small frying pan and add the livers from the hens. Sauté for 3 to 4 minutes and season with cayenne and salt and pepper to taste. Cool and dice. Set aside.

4. Remove the rice from the oven. Stir in the cooked livers, the liver pâté, the truffles, and the parsley. Correct the seasonings, if necessary. Let cool before stuffing the hens.

Roast Turkey

6 TO 10 SERVINGS

1 12- to 18-pound turkey
   Salt
   Freshly ground black pepper
1 large onion, peeled

4 parsley sprigs
½ cup melted butter or
   margarine

1. Preheat the oven to 375 degrees.

2. Sprinkle the turkey inside and out with salt and pepper. Put the onion and parsley in the cavity of the turkey. Do not bother to truss the bird.

3. Put the turkey on a rack in a roasting pan. Add a little water to the bottom of the pan and roast, uncovered, for 15 minutes a pound. Baste occasionally with the pan juices. When the bird has turned brown, cover it with foil, but baste it every so often.

4. During the last 10 minutes of cooking, baste the turkey several times with the melted butter. Remove the turkey from the oven and let it rest, covered loosely with foil, for 20 minutes. Carve and arrange on a platter (see p. 18). Serve with a Stuffing Loaf or Apple Stuffing (see following recipes).

Stuffing Loaf

8 to 10 SERVINGS

2 loaves stale bread, diced
2 to 3 cups Chicken Stock,
   heated (see recipe p. 58)
6 tablespoons butter or
   margarine
2 cups diced onion
2 cups diced celery

6 eggs
   Pinch of poultry seasoning
   Pinch of dried thyme
   Pinch of dried rosemary
   Salt
   Freshly ground black pepper

1. Put the diced bread into a large bowl and pour the hot stock over it. Let sit.

2. Melt the butter in a frying pan and add the onion and celery. Sauté until the onion is golden. Add the onion-celery mixture to the bread with the eggs, poultry seasoning, thyme, and rosemary. Season with salt and pepper to taste and mix well.

3. Pour the stuffing mixture into a large buttered loaf pan and bake alongside turkey for 1 to 1½ hours. Turn out of the pan and slice to serve.

Apple Stuffing

8 to 10 SERVINGS

½ cup butter or margarine
1 small onion, peeled and
    chopped
4 to 5 tart apples, peeled,
    cored, and sliced thin
    Juice of 1 or 2 lemons
    Pinch of sugar
1 teaspoon ground cinnamon

    Salt
    Freshly ground black pepper
½ pound stale bread or rolls,
    diced
4 eggs
1½ cups Chicken Stock (see
    recipe p. 58)

1. Melt the butter in a large frying pan and add the onion. Sauté for 5 or 6 minutes. Add the apples, lemon juice, sugar, cinnamon, and salt and pepper to taste. Cook for a few minutes, stirring occasionally. Add the bread cubes and mix well.

2. Mix the eggs and stock together and pour over the bread mixture. Mix well.

3. Pour the stuffing mixture into a large buttered loaf pan and bake along with the turkey for 30 to 40 minutes, or until crisp and golden on top.

NOTE: If you are baking this by itself, set the oven at 375 degrees.

Roast Duck

6 SERVINGS

3 4-pound ducks
   Salt
   Freshly ground black pepper
   Dried rosemary
3 parsley sprigs

3 apples, peeled, cored, and
   sliced
3 onions, peeled and sliced
   Water or Chicken Stock (see
   recipe p. 58)

1. Preheat the oven to 375 degrees.

2. Sprinkle the ducks inside and out with salt and pepper. Put a pinch of rosemary and a parsley sprig into the cavity of each duck.

3. Put the ducks, breast side down, in a large roasting pan. Put the sliced apples and onions around the ducks in the pan. Pour in enough water to come halfway up the sides of the ducks. Roast for 1½ hours. Add more water as necessary and stir it into the pan juices. Turn the ducks breast side up and roast for 1 to 1½ hours longer, adding more water, if necessary. Remove the ducks to a serving platter and keep them warm.

4. Degrease the sauce and strain it. Serve the sauce over the carved ducks.

Roast Goose

8 TO 10 SERVINGS

1 10- to 14-pound goose
   Salt
   Freshly ground black pepper
   Pinch of dried thyme
1 apple, peeled, cored, and
   sliced

1 onion, peeled and sliced
   Water or Chicken Stock (see
   recipe p. 58)

1. Preheat the oven to 375 degrees.

2. Sprinkle the goose inside and out with salt and pepper. Sprinkle the thyme in the cavity.

3. Put the goose, breast side down, in a roasting pan. Put the sliced apple and onion around the goose in the pan. Pour in enough water to come halfway up the sides of the goose. Roast for 2 to 2½ hours. Add more water as necessary and stir it into the pan juices. Turn the goose breast side up and roast for 1½ to 2 hours longer, or until the meat is tender and the skin is brown. Add more water, if necessary, and stir it into the pan juices. Remove the goose to a serving platter and keep it warm.

4. Degrease the sauce and strain it. Correct the seasonings, if necessary, and serve the sauce with the carved goose. Lingonberry Apples (see recipe p. 203) go nicely with the goose.

7
Fish and Shellfish

Poisson en Papillote and Poached Fish with Zucchini.

Fish is very good for you and it is easy to prepare because it cooks so quickly. It can be stewed, sautéed, pan-fried, or baked and served plain or with a sauce, whatever your preference.

There are a few things you should remember when you buy fish. Really fresh fish has a sweet smell. If the fish you are looking at smells of fish, it is not fresh—so don't buy it. Fish fillets should look shiny and feel firm. If they don't, they've been around for a while, so you shouldn't buy them either.

When you buy a whole fish, check that the eyes are clear, not cloudy or glazed over. The scales should be shiny and the gills should be bright red.

These few tips may not make you popular with your fish man, but he won't be able to sell you an old piece of fish.

Bouillabaisse

6 SERVINGS

¼ cup olive oil
2 leeks, well washed and
   chopped
1 onion, peeled and chopped
2 carrots, trimmed, scraped, and
   chopped
3 stalks fennel, chopped, or 1
   teaspoon fennel seeds
2 stalks celery, trimmed and
   chopped
3 tomatoes, peeled, seeded, and
   diced
2 cloves garlic, peeled and
   minced
   Salt
   Freshly ground black pepper
1 pound clams, cleaned and
   brushed
1 pound mussels, cleaned and
   bearded

½ pound shrimp, peeled and
   deveined
6 small lobster tails
¼ cup Pernod
1 cup dry white wine
½ teaspoon crumbled saffron
   threads
1 bay leaf
1 2-inch strip orange peel
8 cups Fish Stock (see recipe p.
   58) or clam juice
½ pound red snapper or bass
½ pound halibut fillets
½ pound flounder or sole fillets
   Garlic Croutons (see recipe
   p. 159)
   Rouille (see recipe below)

1. Heat the oil in a large heavy pot and add the leeks, onion, carrots, fennel, celery, tomatoes, and garlic and sauté for 5 minutes, stirring occasionally. Season with salt and pepper to taste. Add the clams, mussels, shrimp, and lobster tails. Cover and cook for 5 minutes. Remove the fish to a soup tureen and keep warm.

2. Add the Pernod, white wine, saffron, bay leaf, and orange peel. Stir in the stock and bring to a boil. Add the red snapper, halibut, and flounder and poach until just barely tender. Remove each piece of fish as it is done and keep it warm in the tureen.

3. Correct the seasonings of the soup, if necessary, and pour it over the fish in the tureen. Serve with Garlic Croutons and Rouille.

Rouille

3 to 4 cloves garlic, peeled
3 egg yolks
1 tablespoon lemon juice
1 cup olive oil

1 pimiento, minced
Few drops Tabasco sauce
Salt
Freshly ground black pepper

Purée the garlic in a blender. Add the egg yolks and lemon juice and blend for a few seconds. With the motor running, add the oil slowly. When the ingredients are totally combined, pour the sauce into a small bowl. Stir in the pimiento, Tabasco sauce, and salt and pepper to taste.

Cioppino

6 SERVINGS

4 tablespoons olive oil
1 onion, peeled and chopped
2 cloves garlic, peeled and
  minced
1 celery stalk, trimmed and
  chopped
1 small green pepper, seeded
  and chopped
1 large can Italian plum
  tomatoes
1 cup tomato purée
1 cup dry red wine
1 teaspoon dried basil

1 teaspoon dried oregano
Salt
Freshly ground black pepper
1 dozen clams, cleaned and
  brushed
½ pound shrimp, peeled and
  deveined
3 small lobster tails, cut in half
½ pound scallops
½ pound halibut fillets
½ pound red snapper
½ pound fluke
½ pound bass

1. Heat the oil in a large heavy pot and add the onion and garlic and sauté for 5 minutes, stirring occasionally. Add the celery, green pepper, tomatoes, tomato purée, wine, basil, oregano, and salt and pepper to taste. Bring to a boil and simmer for 1 hour. Correct the seasonings, if necessary.

2. Add the clams and simmer for 5 minutes. Add the rest of the shellfish and fish, cover, and simmer for about 10 minutes, or until the clams have opened and the rest of the fish is cooked. Serve in soup bowls with a good crusty bread and a hearty red wine.

NOTE: The basic sauce for this fish stew can be prepared up to the end of Step 1 and refrigerated for up to 3 days. When you are ready to serve it, just bring it to a boil and follow Step 2 to the end.

Poisson en Papillote

6 SERVINGS

Butter or margarine
6 flounder fillets
3 tomatoes, peeled, seeded, and
   diced
18 asparagus spears, trimmed
3 tablespoons dry white wine

Juice of 1 lemon
Salt
Freshly ground black pepper
4 tablespoons melted butter or
   margarine
6 sprigs parsley

1. Preheat the oven to 350 degrees.

2. For each papillote, cut off a large square of heavy-duty aluminum foil. Butter the center of one side of the foil. Roll one fish fillet, skin side in, and place it on the buttered foil. Add some diced tomatoes and three asparagus spears. Sprinkle with a little wine and lemon juice and season with salt and pepper. Drizzle on a little melted butter and add a parsley sprig.

3. Bring the edges of the foil together over the fish and vegetables. Turn up a few times to seal the edges together, being careful not to pull the foil too tightly over the fish and vegetables. Seal the sides by turning the edges up twice and pressing them together. Make five more papillotes with the rest of the ingredients. Put the packages on a baking sheet as you make them.

4. Bake for 35 to 45 minutes, or until the foil has puffed up well. Serve 1 package per person, to be opened at the table.

Bluefish Provençale

6 SERVINGS

2 to 3 pounds bluefish fillets
    Juice of 2 lemons
    Salt
    Freshly ground black pepper
1 cup bread crumbs

½ cup chopped parsley
½ cup minced onion
4 cloves garlic, peeled and
    minced
2 teaspoons dry mustard

1. Preheat the oven to 350 degrees.
2. Put the fillets in a baking dish and sprinkle them with lemon juice and salt and pepper.
3. Mix the bread crumbs, parsley, onion, garlic, and mustard together in a small bowl. Spread over the fillets.
4. Bake for 20 to 30 minutes, or until the fish flakes easily.

Poached Fish with Zucchini

6 SERVINGS

6 flounder fillets
    Salt
    Freshly ground black pepper
    Juice of 1 lemon
½ cup dry white wine
½ cup water
    Sautéed Zucchini (see recipe
        p. 184)

1 tablespoon cornstarch
    dissolved in 2 tablespoons
    water
2 tablespoons butter or
    margarine (optional)

1. Preheat the oven to 375 degrees.
2. Season the fillets with salt and pepper. Roll them, skin side in, and put them seam side down in a buttered or oiled baking dish. Sprinkle the lemon juice over the fillets and pour the wine and water around them. Bake for 10 or 15 minutes. The fish will turn opaque when done.
3. Put a bed of Sautéed Zucchini in the bottom of a serving dish and lay the rolled fillets on the zucchini. Keep warm.

4. Pour the sauce from the baking dish into a small saucepan and reduce it a little. Thicken the sauce with some of the cornstarch mixture. Add the butter for flavor, if desired, and pour the sauce over the fish. Serve immediately.

Baked Stuffed Fish

6 SERVINGS

8 tablespoons butter or margarine, softened
½ pound mushrooms, sliced
2 cloves garlic, peeled and minced
1 cup bread crumbs
1 egg
Juice of ½ lemon
4 tablespoons chopped parsley
Dash of Pernod

Salt
Freshly ground black pepper
1 3- to 4-pound whole fish, such as striped bass, red snapper, or sea trout, cleaned and boned
1 cup dry white wine
1 cup Fish Stock (see recipe p. 58), clam juice, or water
½ cup heavy cream

1. Melt 2 tablespoons of butter in a small frying pan and add the mushrooms and garlic. Sauté for 5 minutes, stirring. Remove from the heat and let cool a little. Mix in the bread crumbs, egg, lemon juice, the remaining butter, 2 tablespoons of parsley, the Pernod, and salt and pepper to taste.

2. Preheat the oven to 375 degrees.

3. Sprinkle the inside of the fish with salt and pepper. Stuff with the mushroom filling and close the fish with toothpicks. Put the fish in a baking pan and pour in the wine and stock. Bake for 30 minutes, or until the fish flakes easily. Remove the fish from the pan and put it on a serving platter. Remove the toothpicks to make serving easier. Keep the fish warm. To avoid breaking the fish while you are taking it out of the pan, lift it on two long spatulas, one at each end of the fish.

4. Pour the liquid from the baking pan into a small saucepan. Bring the sauce to a boil, add the heavy cream, and reduce the sauce a little. Add the remaining parsley, pour the sauce over the fish, and serve hot.

Fish Quenelles

6 SERVINGS

1 pound flounder, pike, or fluke
   fillets, cut in pieces
6 egg whites
10 slices trimmed white bread,
   soaked in water and
   squeezed dry

cup clarified butter (see
   p. 211)
Salt
Freshly ground white pepper
Fish Stock (see recipe p. 58)

1. Put the fish pieces in the container of a food processor and grind them well. Add the egg whites and mix well. Add the soaked bread and the butter, processing after each addition. Pour the mixture into a small bowl and season with salt and pepper to taste.

2. Form the quenelles as shown on p. 17. Poach them for a few minutes in the simmering stock. Remove the quenelles from the stock with a slotted spoon. Serve with Sauce Alsacienne (see recipe p. 214).

Seafood Timbales

8 SERVINGS

½ cup water
8 tablespoons butter or
   margarine
½ cup all-purpose flour
   Salt
2 eggs
1 pound flounder or fluke fillets,
   cut in pieces
   Freshly ground black pepper
1 cup heavy cream

½ cup diced mushrooms
½ cup diced raw shrimp
½ cup diced lobster meat
½ cup bay scallops
1 teaspoon chopped truffles
   (optional)
   Beurre Blanc (see recipe
   p. 217)
2 tablespoons chopped parsley

1. Put the water and 4 tablespoons of butter in a saucepan. Bring to a boil and add the flour and a pinch of salt all at once. Stir over

medium heat until smooth and dry. Remove the pan from the heat and beat in the eggs one at a time. Beat well after adding each egg. Let the *pâte à choux* cool completely.

2. Put the fish pieces in the container of a food processor and grind them well. Add the cooled *pâte à choux* and blend in. Remove the mixture to a bowl and season with salt and pepper to taste. Set the bowl in a larger bowl filled with chopped ice. When the mixture is well chilled, gradually stir in the cream and set aside.

3. Melt the remaining butter in a frying pan and add the mushrooms. Sauté over high heat until the mushrooms give up most of their liquid. Add the shrimp, lobster, and scallops and season with salt and pepper. Sauté for 1 or 2 minutes only. Cool the mixture completely.

4. Combine the fish-*pâte à choux* mixture with the fish-mushroom mixture and correct seasonings, if necessary. Add the truffles, if desired.

5. Preheat the oven to 375 degrees.

6. Butter eight small timbale molds very well. Fill the molds two-thirds full with the fish mixture. Put the timbales into a roasting pan and pour in enough boiling water to come halfway up the sides of the molds. Bake for 25 to 30 minutes. Turn the timbales out onto individual serving plates, spoon some Beurre Blanc sauce around the timbales, sprinkle with parsley, and serve immediately.

Mélange of Seafood

6 SERVINGS

1 ounce bean thread or cellophane noodles (available in Oriental food stores)
2 tablespoons butter or margarine
2 celery stalks, trimmed and sliced thin
2 carrots, trimmed, scraped, and julienned (see p. 5)
2 cups bok choy, cut into ½-inch-thick slices
1 cup sliced mushrooms
Salt
Freshly ground black pepper
½ pound shrimp, shelled
½ pound scallops
¾ cup Chicken Stock (see recipe p. 58)
¾ cup dry white wine
1 dozen clams, cleaned and brushed
1 dozen mussels, cleaned and bearded
1 to 2 tablespoons soy sauce

1. Put the bean thread in a bowl and cover it with warm water. Let it soak for 1 hour, then drain and cut it into 1-inch lengths.

2. Melt the butter in a frying pan and add the celery, carrots, bok choy, and mushrooms and sauté for 5 minutes, stirring occasionally. Season with salt and pepper to taste. Add the shrimp and scallops and sauté for 1 or 2 minutes only. Remove from the heat and set aside.

3. Put the stock and white wine into a saucepan and bring to a boil. Add the clams and mussels, cover, and steam them until their shells open a little. Remove the shellfish with a slotted spoon and set aside in a bowl. Continue to boil the liquid until it is reduced by half.

4. Preheat the oven to 375 degrees.

5. Cut off six large squares of heavy-duty aluminum foil. Put some of the sautéed vegetables and fish and bean thread in the center of each piece of foil. Put 1 fish fillet over each portion of vegetables and bean threads. Season with salt and pepper, and distribute the clams and mussels equally among the portions.

6. Mix the reduced stock with the soy sauce and pour the sauce over each of the portions.

7. Bring the edges of the foil together over the fish and vegetables. Turn down a few times to seal the edges together. Don't seal the foil too tightly over the fish and vegetables because the clam and mussel shells will need space to open. Seal the sides by turning the edges up twice and pressing them together.

8. Bake for 30 to 35 minutes, or until the foil has puffed up well. Serve 1 package per person, to be opened at the table.

Fillet of Pike in Cream Sauce

6 SERVINGS

4 tablespoons butter or margarine
1 onion, peeled and chopped
2 pounds pike or fluke fillets, or an equal amount of any other firm, white-meat, freshwater fish
Salt
Freshly ground black pepper
1 bay leaf

½ cup dry white wine
½ cup Fish Stock (see recipe p. 58), bottled clam juice, or water
1 cup heavy cream
2 tablespoons chopped parsley
2 tablespoons chopped fresh dill
Pinch of ground nutmeg
Juice of ½ lemon

1. Melt the butter in a large frying pan and add the onion. Sauté for 3 to 4 minutes and add the fish fillets. Season with salt and pepper to taste and add the bay leaf, white wine, and stock. Cover and simmer for 20 minutes. Remove the fish carefully to a serving platter and keep it warm.

2. Reduce the poaching liquid in the frying pan by half. Add the cream, parsley, and dill and reduce by half again. Season with the nutmeg and lemon juice and pour the sauce over the fish. Serve with rice or noodles.

Pike in Beer Batter

6 SERVINGS

2 pounds pike or fluke fillets, or
    an equal amount of any
    other firm, white-meat,
    freshwater fish
Salt
Freshly ground black pepper

Lemon juice to taste
Oil for deep frying
Flour for dredging
Beer Batter (see recipe p. 139)
Sauce Ravigote (see recipe
    p. 200)

1. Cut the fish into bite-size pieces and season it with salt, pepper, and lemon juice. Let sit for a few minutes.

2. Begin heating the oil. Put the flour on a large square of wax paper.

3. When the oil is hot, dip the fish pieces in the flour and then in the Beer Batter. Drop the pieces into the hot fat and fry until golden brown. As the pieces turn golden brown, remove them to a platter lined with paper towels. Serve with Sauce Ravigote.

Salmon with Sorrel Sauce

6 SERVINGS

4 shallots, peeled and minced
1 cup dry white wine
1 cup dry vermouth
2 cups Fish Stock (see recipe
    p. 58) or bottled clam juice
1 cup heavy cream
    Handful of sorrel, julienned,
    blanched, and drained well

1 teaspoon lemon juice
Salt
Freshly ground black pepper
12 very thin slices fresh salmon
6 tablespoons vegetable oil
4 tablespoons butter or
    margarine, cut in small
    pieces

1. Put the shallots, wine, vermouth, and stock into the top of a double boiler. Bring to a boil and reduce the liquid to one third of its original volume. Add the cream and reduce a little more. Add the sorrel, lemon juice, and salt and pepper to taste. Cover and keep the sauce warm over hot water while you prepare the fish.

2. Sprinkle the fish with salt and pepper.

3. Heat the oil in a skillet and add the fish slices. Sauté for a few seconds on each side.

4. Whisk the butter into the hot sauce and, when it is fully combined, put a few spoons of sauce on each serving plate. Top the sauce with two slices of sautéed fish and serve immediately.

Salmon Surprise

6 SERVINGS

6 slices fresh salmon, about 6 ounces each	6 tablespoons butter or margarine
Salt	1 cup dry white wine
Freshly ground black pepper	6 tarragon leaves
Flour for dredging	1 cup heavy cream

1. Season the salmon with salt and pepper and dredge in the flour.

2. Melt the butter in a large frying pan and add the salmon slices. Sauté for about 5 minutes on each side. Remove the fish to a serving platter and keep it warm.

3. Add the wine to the pan and reduce by half. Add the fresh tarragon and cook for a few seconds. Pour in the cream and reduce the sauce by half again. Correct the seasonings, if necessary, and pour the sauce over the fish. Serve immediately.

Sole Meunière

6 SERVINGS

6 whole Dover sole, skinned and
   trimmed
Salt
4 lemons
   Flour for dredging

4 tablespoons vegetable oil
4 tablespoons butter or
   margarine, cut in small
   pieces
3 tablespoons chopped parsley

1. Sprinkle the fish with salt and squeeze the juice of 3 of the lemons over the fish. Let sit for a few minutes.
2. Dredge the fish in the flour and shake off any excess flour.
3. Heat the oil in a large frying pan and add the fish. Sauté for 2 to 3 minutes on each side. When the fish is almost cooked, add the butter to the pan and sauté for 3 minutes longer. Remove the fish to a serving platter and keep warm.
4. Squeeze the juice of the remaining lemon into the frying pan and add the parsley. Swirl the pan so that everything is combined and pour the sauce over the fish. Serve immediately.

Nouvelle Cuisine Fish Fillets

6 SERVINGS

6 tablespoons butter or
   margarine
1 large onion, peeled and sliced
1 celery root, diced, or 3 celery
   stalks, sliced
4 carrots, trimmed, scraped, and
   sliced

6 fish fillets, such as sole,
   snapper, bass, or flounder
Salt
Freshly ground black pepper
½ cup dry white wine
Lemon juice to taste (optional)
3 tablespoons chopped parsley

1. Melt 3 tablespoons of butter in a frying pan. Add the onion, celery root, and carrots and sauté for about 10 minutes, or until the vegetables are soft. Transfer the cooked vegetables to the bottom of a small buttered baking dish.
2. Preheat the oven to 375 degrees.

3. Sprinkle the fish fillets with salt and pepper and roll them up, skin side in. Place the rolled fillets, seam side down, on top of the vegetable bedding. Sprinkle the wine over the fish and cover the dish tightly with foil. Bake for 8 to 10 minutes, or until the fish flakes easily. Remove the fish rolls from the oven and transfer them carefully to a serving platter. Keep them warm.

4. Purée the vegetables and liquid from the baking dish in a food mill, food processor, or blender. Pour the puréed sauce into a small saucepan and reheat. Add the remaining butter, lemon juice, and chopped parsley. Correct the seasonings, if necessary. (If the sauce is too thick, add a little white wine.) Pour the hot sauce over the fish and serve immediately.

Rainbow Trout Meunière

6 SERVINGS

6 rainbow trout, 12 to 16 ounces each	6 tablespoons butter or margarine
Salt	Flour for dredging
Freshly ground black pepper	3 tablespoons chopped parsley
Juice of 3 lemons	6 lemon slices
Few drops of Worcestershire sauce (optional)	

1. Sprinkle the trout with salt and pepper and squeeze the lemon juice over them. Sprinkle on the Worcestershire sauce. Let the fish sit for 10 to 15 minutes, turning them occasionally.

2. Melt the butter in a large frying pan. Put the flour on a large square of wax paper.

3. When the butter is hot, dredge the fish in the flour and then sauté them for about 6 minutes on each side. Transfer the fish to a platter lined with paper towels.

4. Add the marinating liquid to the pan with the parsley. Swirl it around until hot and pour the sauce over the fish. Garnish with the lemon slices and serve immediately.

NOTE: Don't forget to remove the paper towels before you pour the sauce over the fish.

Poached Rainbow Trout

6 SERVINGS

12 cups water
2 small carrots, trimmed and
   scraped
2 celery stalks, trimmed
1 onion, peeled

1 bay leaf
¾ cup red wine vinegar
Salt to taste
6 rainbow trout, about 14 to 16
   ounces each (see Note)

Combine all the ingredients except the trout in a large pot. Bring to a boil, lower the heat to a simmer, and add the fish. Cover and simmer the fish for 10 minutes. Remove the fish with a slotted spoon, being careful not to damage the skin. Serve immediately with Horseradish Cream (see recipe p. 216) or browned butter.

NOTE: If you are using fresh trout, clean them lightly under cold running water so that the slippery layer above the skin stays intact. This layer, if it is whole, will give the fish a nice blue color after it is poached. If you are using thawed frozen trout, cook them in a single layer in a large pan. Frozen trout will not have the blue color of the fresh fish.

Mussels in White Wine Sauce

6 SERVINGS

5 pounds mussels
2 tablespoons butter or
   margarine
1 onion, peeled and chopped
1 cup dry white wine

1 cup water
2 tablespoons chopped parsley
1 teaspoon salt
1 dried red chili pepper

1. Clean the mussels well and beard them.
2. Melt the butter in a pot big enough to hold the mussels when they open. Add the onion and sauté for 5 minutes, stirring often. Do not let the onion brown; it should just be soft. Add the wine, water,

parsley, salt, and chili pepper. Bring to a boil and add the drained mussels. Bring to a boil again, cover the pot, and cook the mussels over medium heat until their shells open wide, about 10 minutes. Discard any unopened mussels and serve the mussels in deep soup bowls with the sauce and rye bread on the side.

Coquilles Parisienne

6 SERVINGS

7 tablespoons butter or margarine
4 tablespoons all-purpose flour
1 cup milk
1 cup Fish Stock (see recipe p. 58) or bottled clam juice
Salt
Freshly ground black pepper

1 cup grated Gruyère cheese
2 shallots, peeled and minced
¼ pound mushrooms, sliced
1 pound bay scallops
½ cup dry white wine
Juice of ½ lemon
1 chopped truffle (optional)
½ cup grated Parmesan cheese

1. Melt 4 tablespoons of butter in a saucepan and add the flour all at once. Stir until the mixture is smooth and creamy. Cook for 2 minutes, stirring. Remove and let the *roux* cool.

2. Heat the milk and the stock together. When it is hot, pour it slowly into the cooled *roux*, stirring constantly. Season with salt and pepper to taste, bring to a simmer, and cook for 20 minutes. The sauce should be very thick. Add the cheese and stir until it is melted completely. Set the sauce aside.

3. Melt 2 tablespoons of butter in a frying pan and add the shallots and mushrooms. Sauté for 5 minutes. Season with salt and pepper and add the scallops, wine, and lemon juice. Cook, stirring occasionally, for 3 minutes, or until the wine is reduced a little. Add the reserved sauce and the truffle and mix well.

4. Preheat the oven to 400 degrees.

5. Spoon the mixture evenly into 6 scallop shells. Sprinkle the grated cheese over the top and dot with the remaining butter.

6. Bake for 8 to 10 minutes, or until hot and browned on top. Serve immediately.

Sautéed Bay Scallops

6 SERVINGS

6 tablespoons butter or margarine	1½ cups finely chopped celery
	Salt to taste
1½ pounds bay scallops	¾ cup dry white wine
1½ cups finely chopped carrots	¼ cup chopped parsley

Heat a frying pan and, when it is hot, add the butter. When the butter has melted and begun to sizzle, add the scallops and stir. First add the carrots and stir, then the celery and stir. Sprinkle with salt and stir in the wine. Cook for 5 minutes, stirring occasionally. Sprinkle with parsley and serve immediately.

Sautéed Sea Scallops

6 SERVINGS

6 tablespoons butter or margarine	Freshly ground black pepper
	Juice of 2 lemons
1½ pounds sea scallops	¼ cup chopped parsley
Salt	

Heat a frying pan and, when it is hot, add the butter. When the butter has melted and begins to sizzle, add the scallops and sauté them for 5 minutes, turning them at least once. As the scallops cook, season them with salt and pepper. At the very last moment, sprinkle on the lemon juice and chopped parsley. Serve immediately.

Fritto Misto

6 SERVINGS

Fish:

18 clams, shelled
24 mussels, shelled
1 pound shrimp, shelled and deveined

1½ pounds fish fillets, such as halibut, flounder, or fluke, cut into bite-size pieces

Beer Batter:

2 cups all-purpose flour
1 tablespoon sugar
Pinch of salt
2 tablespoons oil

4 egg yolks
4 egg whites, stiffly beaten
½ cup beer

Oil for deep frying

1. Prepare the fish and have it ready to go into the batter.

2. Combine all the ingredients for the batter, mixing carefully so that you get a very light consistency.

3. Heat the oil to 350 degrees. Dip the prepared fish into the batter, and drop it into the hot oil, a few pieces at a time. As each piece of fish turns golden brown, transfer it to a platter lined with paper towels so that it drains. When all the fish is cooked, serve it immediately with Tomato Sauce (see recipe p. 217).

Joahin's Shrimp

6 SERVINGS

36 large shrimp, peeled and deveined, but with tails left on
3 cloves garlic, peeled and crushed
¼ teaspoon paprika
Juice of 2 lemons
8 tablespoons butter or margarine
1½ cups minced onion

4 tablespoons brandy
1 cup dry white wine
1½ cups peeled, seeded, and diced tomatoes
1½ cups ketchup
Salt
Freshly ground black pepper
1 cup heavy cream
3 tablespoons chopped parsley
1 teaspoon Pernod

1. Butterfly the shrimp by cutting them almost in half following the cut already made when you deveined them.

2. Combine the garlic, paprika, and lemon juice in a bowl and add the shrimp. Toss the shrimp gently with two spoons until they are coated with the mixture. Let them sit for 10 minutes.

3. Melt the butter in a frying pan. When it is hot, add the shrimp and sauté them, stirring, for 3 minutes. Add the onion and cook until it is soft.

4. Pour the brandy over the shrimp and set it aflame. (Be careful not to burn yourself.) When the flames die down, remove the shrimp from the pan and keep them warm.

5. Pour the wine into the frying pan and stir it around with a wooden spoon to scrape up all the browned-on bits in the pan. Add the tomatoes, ketchup, and salt and pepper to taste. Cook over medium heat until the sauce has thickened. Add the cream and cook down again until the sauce is thick. Sprinkle the sauce with a little more paprika, the chopped parsley, and the Pernod. Return the shrimp to the pan and heat them in the sauce for 1 or 2 minutes. Serve at once over Rice Pilaf (see recipe p. 155).

8

Pasta, Pasta Sauces, Rice, and Dumplings

Potato Dumplings, Spätzle, and Spanish Rice.

Here are some good side dishes and main dishes. You really should try my easy recipe for homemade pasta. Once you do, you'll want to eat it all the time.

Pasta Fresca

1½ POUNDS

2½ cups all-purpose flour   5 eggs, lightly beaten
    Pinch of salt   2 teaspoons oil

1. Mix the flour with the salt and put it in a mound in the center of a large cutting board. Make a well in the center of the flour and put the eggs and oil into the well.

2. Begin to mix the dough by adding the flour to the eggs and oil slowly with your fingers until the liquid is all mixed in.

3. Knead the dough by pushing it away from you with the palms of your hands. First you push the dough away from you, then fold it in half, turn it over, and push again. Do this until the dough is stiff and shiny. Let the dough rest for about 30 minutes.

4. Set your pasta machine to the thickest setting. Put the dough through the machine once. Keep resetting the machine and putting the dough through until you get the thickness you want. Flour the dough as you go along so that it doesn't stick to the machine. You will have to cut the dough into smaller portions as the setting on the machine is lowered.

5. Cut the pasta into the size you want and let it sit for 5 minutes on a towel or cookie sheet that has been sprinkled with flour. You can also sprinkle the cut noodles lightly with flour so they do not stick together. Cover them with another towel.

NOTE: The pasta dough can be mixed in a food processor, if you wish. Just put all the ingredients into the container of the processor and blend, turning the machine on and off, until the dough is formed. Let it rest and then proceed to roll the dough through the pasta machine.

Pasta Verde
1½ POUNDS

1 recipe Pasta Fresca (see recipe p. 142)

1 10-ounce box frozen chopped spinach, thawed and squeezed dry

Add the spinach to the dough just before you begin to knead it. Incorporate it into the dough as well as you can—it will get more worked in as you knead.

COOKING HOMEMADE PASTA

Homemade pasta doesn't take as long to cook as the boxed varieties you buy in a store. Make sure you use lots of boiling salted water and that you stir the pasta while it cooks. Test after 2 or 3 minutes of boiling to see if it is done.

When you cook sheet pasta, such as lasagne, have a bowl of ice water next to the pot. Remove the pasta with a slotted spoon and put it into the bowl to stop the cooking process.

Pasta Verde with Prosciutto

6 SERVINGS

4 tablespoons butter or margarine

1 cup diced prosciutto

½ recipe Pasta Verde (see recipe above), or 1½ pounds dried spinach pasta

4 tablespoons chopped parsley
Salt
Freshly ground black pepper
¾ cup heavy cream
4 eggs, lightly beaten
½ cup grated Parmesan cheese

1. Melt the butter in a large pan and add the prosciutto. Sauté for 4 to 5 minutes, stirring occasionally. Remove from the heat and set aside.

2. Cook the pasta in boiling salted water until it is *al dente*. Drain and add to the sautéed prosciutto. Add the parsley, salt and pepper to taste, and the cream. Toss well and put over very low heat until it is very hot. Remove from the heat and add the eggs, tossing to distribute them well. Serve immediately and pass the cheese separately.

Pasta Primavera

6 SERVINGS

1 cup string beans, cut into 1-inch lengths
10 tablespoons butter or margarine
½ cup pine nuts
1 cup sliced mushrooms
1 cup broccoli flowerets
1 cup fresh peas
1 cup sliced zucchini
1 cup cauliflower flowerets
4 large tomatoes, peeled, seeded, and diced
2 cloves garlic, peeled and crushed
2 tablespoons chopped parsley
2 teaspoons dried basil, or 2 tablespoons chopped fresh basil
Salt
Freshly ground black pepper
1 pound linguini
6 quarts water
1½ cups heavy cream
½ cup grated Parmesan cheese

1. Cook the string beans in boiling salted water until they are just crisp. Drain, refresh under cold running water, drain again, and set aside.

2. Melt 2 tablespoons of butter in a large frying pan and add the pine nuts. Sauté, stirring constantly, until the nuts are a light golden brown. Remove the nuts with a slotted spoon and set them aside.

3. Add the string beans, mushrooms, broccoli, peas, zucchini, and cauliflower to the skillet and sauté, stirring constantly, for 3 minutes. Add 2 tablespoons of water to the pan, cover, and steam the vegetables for 5 minutes. (The vegetables should be very crisp.)

4. Add the tomatoes, garlic, parsley, and basil and mix well. Cook for 2 minutes, then stir in the reserved pine nuts and season the mixture with salt and pepper to taste.

5. While the sauce is cooking, bring the water to a boil. Add 2 tablespoons of salt and the linguini. Cook, stirring occasionally, until the pasta is *al dente*.

6. Melt the remaining butter in a very large pan. Drain the cooked pasta and add it to the pan. Toss so that the pasta is coated with the melted butter. Add the cream and cheese and toss again. Add the vegetable sauce and mix well. Serve immediately.

NOTE: This recipe calls for fresh vegetables in season. Substitutions can be made, depending on what you like and what is available at the market.

Pasta with Zucchini

6 SERVINGS

6 zucchini
  Salt
6 tablespoons butter or
    margarine
½ cup finely minced onion
1 clove garlic, peeled and
    crushed
  Freshly ground black pepper

1 teaspoon dried basil, or 1
    tablespoon minced fresh
    basil
1 pound linguini or penne
½ to 1 cup heavy cream
½ cup grated Parmesan or
    Asiago cheese

1. Wash and trim the zucchini, but do not peel them. Dice the zucchini, put them in a bowl, and salt them well. Let the zucchini sit for 30 minutes, then rinse and drain them well.

2. Melt 3 tablespoons of butter in a frying pan and sauté the onion for 3 minutes, or until it is soft. Add the garlic, zucchini, salt and pepper to taste, and the basil. Sauté, stirring often, until the zucchini are tender.

4. Cook the pasta in boiling salted water until it is *al dente*.

5. While the pasta is cooking, heat the remaining butter with the cream in a very large saucepan. Drain the pasta and add it to the saucepan with the cream and butter. Add the grated cheese and toss well. Add the zucchini and toss again. Serve immediately with extra cheese, if desired, and freshly ground black pepper.

Straw and Hay

6 SERVINGS

8 tablespoons butter or
    margarine
1 pound mushrooms, diced
6 to 8 quarts water
    Salt
    Freshly ground black pepper
1 cup frozen peas, thawed and
    drained

½ recipe Pasta Fresca (see recipe
    p. 142), cut into linguini
½ recipe Pasta Verde (see recipe
    p. 146), cut into linguini
1 cup heavy cream
1 cup grated Parmesan cheese

1. Melt 2 tablespoons of butter in a frying pan and add the diced mushrooms. Sauté the mushrooms for 5 to 10 minutes, or until they have given up most of their liquid. Season the mushrooms with salt and pepper as they cook. Add the peas and cook for 3 minutes. Set aside.

2. Bring the water to a boil and add 2 tablespoons of salt. When the water returns to the boil, add the two kinds of pasta and cook, stirring, for a few minutes, or until the pasta is *al dente*. (Remember homemade pasta doesn't take very long to get to that stage.)

3. While the pasta is cooking, heat the remaining butter with the cream in a very large saucepan. Drain the pasta and add it to the saucepan with the cream and butter. Add half the cheese and toss well. Add the mushrooms and peas and toss again. Correct the seasonings, if necessary. You can add the remaining cheese at this point, or serve it separately. Serve the dish immediately.

NOTE: If the sauce is too thick, you can thin it with a little cream or milk.

Lasagne

9 SERVINGS

2 pounds ricotta cheese
2 to 3 eggs
½ cup chopped parsley
1 pound Parmesan or Locatelli
    cheese
    Salt
    Freshly ground black pepper
8 cups Tomato Sauce (see
    recipe p. 152)
1 pound lasagne noodles,
    cooked *al dente* and
    drained

1 1-pound mozzarella cheese,
    diced
8 tablespoons butter or
    margarine
20 meatballs from Tomato
    Sauce
2 pounds cooked sausage from
    Tomato Sauce, sliced

1. Mix the ricotta, eggs, parsley, and ½ cup grated Parmesan cheese in a large bowl. The easiest way to do this is to beat the ingredients with a fork until they are well combined. Season with salt and pepper to taste.

2. Use a 9- by 13-inch baking dish to make the lasagne. Add a layer of Tomato Sauce and spread it around the bottom of the dish. Then add the noodles in one layer, overlapping them a little so the filling won't seep out. Spread half of the ricotta mixture over the noodles. Use a wooden spoon to even the layer. Top the ricotta with half of the diced mozzarella and half of the butter cut into small pieces. Distribute half the meatballs and half the sausage evenly over the cheese. Pour about ½ cup of sauce over the top.

3. Make another layer of noodles and add the ricotta mixture, mozzarella, butter, meatballs, and sausage as you did previously. Top with more sauce. Add a final layer of noodles and cover them well with sauce. Sprinkle with some grated cheese.

4. Bake in a 375-degree oven for about 1 hour. If the dish starts to brown too fast, cover it with foil, but it should be browned nicely when you take it out of the oven. Let the lasagne rest for 10 minutes before you cut and serve it. Serve with additional sauce and grated cheese.

Noodles with Ham and Cheese

6 SERVINGS

1 pound egg noodles, cooked *al dente* and drained
1 cup cooked diced ham
½ cup grated Swiss cheese
4 eggs, beaten
1 cup heavy cream

Pinch of ground nutmeg
Salt
Freshly ground black pepper
Bread crumbs
Butter or margarine

1. Preheat the oven to 375 degrees.

2. Put the cooked noodles into a large mixing bowl and add the ham and cheese. Toss to mix well.

3. Beat the eggs with the cream until they are well combined. Pour the mixture over the noodles and combine them well. Season with the nutmeg and salt and pepper to taste.

4. Pour the noodle mixture into a well-buttered 2-quart soufflé dish. Sprinkle with bread crumbs and dot with little pieces of butter. Bake for 30 minutes, or until brown on top and heated through.

Noodles with Shallot Butter

6 SERVINGS

4 tablespoons butter or margarine
3 tablespoons minced shallots
1 pound egg noodles, cooked *al dente* and drained

3 tablespoons chopped parsley
Salt
Freshly ground black pepper

Melt the butter in a large frying pan and add the shallots. Sauté, stirring, until the shallots are golden. Add the noodles, toss well to heat them through, mix in the parsley, and season with salt and pepper to taste. Serve immediately.

Sweet Noodle Soufflé

6 SERVINGS

4½ cups milk
¾ cup sugar
½ teaspoon vanilla extract
Peel of 1 lemon
12 ounces egg noodles
6 egg yolks, beaten

¾ cup raisins, soaked in warm
    water to cover or rum
¾ cup diced, peeled apple
6 egg whites
    Butter or margarine

1. Bring the milk, sugar, vanilla, and lemon peel to a boil in a large saucepan. Add the noodles and cook until they are just tender. Pour the mixture into a large heatproof bowl and cool. As the noodles and milk cool, they will form a thick custard.

2. Stir the beaten egg yolks into the custard with a wooden spoon, being careful not to break up the noodles. Drain the raisins and add them and the apples to the custard.

3. Preheat the oven to 375 degrees.

4. Beat the egg whites until they are stiff and fold them into the noodle mixture completely. Pour into a buttered 3-quart soufflé dish. Dot the top of the custard with small pieces of butter and bake for 30 minutes, or until there is a nice brown crust on top. Serve as a main dish with a dried fruit compote on the side.

NOTE: Make sure that you use only the yellow part of the lemon peel. This way the milk will not curdle.

Pesto

1 cup fresh basil leaves, washed
    and dried
6 sprigs parsley
½ cup pine nuts or slivered
    almonds
2 cloves garlic, peeled and
    mashed

⅓ cup grated Parmesan cheese
⅓ cup grated Pecorino or
    Romano cheese
4 tablespoons olive oil
4 tablespoons butter or
    margarine, softened
¼ teaspoon salt

Put all the ingredients into the container of a blender or food processor and blend until they form a smooth paste. Put the paste in a jar with a lid and store in the refrigerator. It will keep about a week.

NOTE: Besides being good on pasta, Pesto can be used to flavor other dishes, or it can be spread on slices of French or Italian bread and toasted.

Tomato Sauce with Meat (Bolognese Sauce)

3 tablespoons Garlic Oil (see
    recipe p. 220)
1 cup chopped onion
1 clove garlic, peeled and
    minced
1 pound ground round or chuck
½ cup Beef, Veal, or Chicken
    Stock (see recipes pp. 56,
    57, and 58)

½ cup tomato purée or tomato
    paste
1 teaspoon dried oregano
    Pinch of ground nutmeg
    Salt
    Freshly ground black pepper

Heat the oil in a large frying pan and add the onion and garlic. Sauté for 5 to 6 minutes, or until the onion is soft. Add the ground meat and sauté until it loses its red color. Break the meat up with a wooden spoon as it cooks so that it doesn't lump together. Add the stock, tomato purée, oregano, and nutmeg. Stir in well and season with salt and pepper to taste. Cover and cook over low heat for 20 to 30 minutes. This sauce is very good with little macaroni shells and grated Romano cheese.

Red Clam Sauce

ENOUGH FOR 1½ POUNDS PASTA

60 littleneck clams in the shells, or 2 cups canned whole clams, drained, with juice reserved
½ cup olive oil
2 cloves garlic, peeled and minced

½ cup chopped parsley
1 tablespoon dried oregano
3 cups Tomato Sauce (see recipe p. 217)

1. Clean the clams well (see p. 260), open them, and make sure you catch all the juice.

2. Heat the oil and add the garlic. Sauté for a few minutes, making sure you do not burn the garlic. Add the reserved clam juice, chopped parsley, and oregano and cook for 10 minutes. Add the fresh clams and cook for 5 minutes.

3. Add the Tomato Sauce and blend well. Cook just to heat through. Serve with linguini but no cheese.

NOTE: Be careful not to cook the clams too long or they will taste like rubber. If you are using canned clams, add them with the Tomato Sauce at the end. They just need to be heated up.

Tomato Sauce with Meatballs and Sausage

4 tablespoons olive oil
1 large onion, peeled and
    minced
2 cloves garlic, peeled and
    minced
2 large cans Italian plum
    tomatoes
5 small cans tomato paste
2 large cans tomato purée
2 cups water
½ cup chopped parsley
2 tablespoons dried oregano
¼ cup chopped fresh basil
    leaves, or 2 tablespoons
    dried basil

2 bay leaves
6 tablespoons grated Parmesan
    cheese
  Salt
  Freshly ground black pepper
2 to 3 pounds Italian sausage
    links, hot and sweet mixed
20 small Meatballs (see recipe
    below)
2 to 3 pork neck bones,
    browned in a little oil
½ cup Pepperoni slices
    (optional)

1. Heat the oil in a large pot. Add the onion and garlic and sauté until the onion is translucent. Be careful not to burn the garlic. Add the tomatoes, tomato paste, tomato purée, and water and stir well. Bring to a boil, stirring occasionally. When the sauce is just boiling, add the parsley, oregano, basil, bay leaves, cheese, and salt and pepper to taste. Stir in well and bring back to a boil.

2. When the sauce is boiling again, add the sausage links, meatballs, and neck bones one at a time, trying not to pile them up on one another. Do not stir the sauce or you will break up the meatballs. Lower the heat, cover the pot, and cook for ½ hour.

3. Stir in the Pepperoni, if desired, and continue to cook the sauce for 2 to 2½ hours longer, stirring occasionally so that the sauce and meats do not stick to the bottom of the pot. Taste the sauce about halfway through the cooking time. If it is too acidy, add a pinch or two of sugar. Don't add too much at one time. Let the sauce cook for a while before you taste it for acidity again.

NOTE: You will have to skim the fat and froth from the top of the sauce as it rises. Just keep scooping it up and throwing it away until no more fat comes to the top.

Meatballs

20 SMALL MEATBALLS

⅔ pound ground pork
⅔ pound ground veal
⅔ pound ground beef
1 medium-size onion, peeled
   and minced
½ cup chopped parsley
5 slices trimmed white bread,
   soaked in water and
   squeezed dry

3 eggs
  Pinch of ground nutmeg
  Salt
  Freshly ground black pepper

Combine all the ingredients in a large mixing bowl, mixing with your hand until you have a smooth paste. Form the meatballs by moistening your hands with cool water and rolling small portions of the mixture between your palms.

Calamari with Tomato Sauce

ENOUGH FOR 1½ POUNDS PASTA

4 tablespoons olive oil
2 cloves garlic, peeled
1 cup minced onion
2 pounds squid, cleaned and cut
   into ½-inch dice
4 tablespoons tomato paste
½ cup dry white wine

½ cup water
2 tablespoons chopped parsley
2 tablespoons chopped fresh
   basil, or 1 tablespoon dried
   basil
  Salt
  Freshly ground black pepper

Heat the oil in a large saucepan and add the garlic. Sauté for a few minutes, making sure the garlic doesn't burn. Add the onion and sauté for 5 minutes. Add the squid, tomato paste, wine, and water and mix well. Stir in the parsley, basil, and salt and pepper to taste. Bring to a boil, cover, lower the heat, and simmer for 30 to 40 minutes or until the squid is tender. Serve with linguini but no cheese.

Paella

3 tablespoons oil
1 large onion, peeled and
    chopped
2 cloves garlic, peeled and
    minced
1 small chicken, cut up (see
    p. 8)
½ pound boneless pork, diced
½ pound Italian sausage or
    Chorizo, sliced
  Salt
  Freshly ground black pepper
2 cups rice
4 cups Chicken Stock (see
    recipe p. 58)

Pinch of saffron threads
1 bay leaf
2 tomatoes, peeled, seeded, and
    diced
12 shelled and deveined shrimp
2 lobster tails, cut into 1½-inch-
    thick slices
12 mussels, cleaned and bearded
12 clams, cleaned and brushed
1 cup frozen peas, thawed and
    drained
½ cup chopped parsley

1. Preheat the oven to 375 degrees.

2. Heat the oil in a large ovenproof frying pan or paella pan. Add the onion and garlic and sauté for 5 minutes, stirring occasionally. Add the chicken, pork, and sausage and brown them well on all sides. Season with salt and pepper to taste. Add the rice and stir to coat the rice with the oil. Add the stock, saffron, and bay leaf. Bring to a boil on top of the stove and then bake, covered, for 15 minutes.

3. Add the tomatoes and stir them in. Distribute the shrimp, lobster, mussels, and clams decoratively throughout the pan, pushing them into the rice mixture so they are partially buried. Sprinkle the peas over the top. Cover again and bake for 10 minutes.

4. Remove the cover and bake for 5 minutes longer. Sprinkle with parsley and serve immediately.

Rice Pilaf

6 SERVINGS

3 tablespoons butter or
   margarine
1 small onion, peeled and
   minced
1 cup rice

2 cups Chicken Stock, heated
   (see recipe p. 58)
Salt
Freshly ground black pepper

1. Preheat the oven to 375 degrees.
2. Melt the butter in an ovenproof pot. Add the onion and sauté
for 5 minutes, or until it is translucent. Add the rice and cook and stir
to coat the rice with the butter. Add the stock, season with salt and
pepper to taste, and bring to a boil. Cover and bake for 18 to 20
minutes.

Tomato Rice Pilaf

6 SERVINGS

3 tablespoons butter or
   margarine
1 small onion, peeled and
   minced
1 cup rice
2 cups Chicken Stock, heated
   (see recipe p. 58)

Salt
Freshly ground black pepper
1 cup peeled, seeded, and diced
   tomatoes
1 tablespoon tomato paste or
   tomato purée (optional)

1. Preheat the oven to 375 degrees.
2. Melt the butter in an ovenproof pot. Add the onion and sauté
for 5 minutes, or until it is translucent. Add the rice and cook and stir
to coat the rice with the butter. Add the stock, season with salt and
pepper to taste, and bring to a boil. Cover and bake for 18 to 20 minutes. Stir in the tomatoes. Add the tomato paste or purée if the fresh
tomatoes don't have much flavor. Correct the seasonings, if necessary.

Spanish Rice

6 SERVINGS

2 tablespoons oil
1 cup diced onions
3 chicken thighs
3 chicken drumsticks
½ pound boneless pork, diced
2 to 3 Italian hot or sweet
    sausages, sliced

4 cups Chicken Stock (see
    recipe p. 58)

Salt
Freshly ground black pepper
2 tomatoes, cored, peeled, and
    quartered
1 cup frozen peas, thawed and
    drained
1 cup broccoli or cauliflower
    flowerets
12 clams, washed and brushed
12 mussels, washed and bearded

1. Preheat the oven to 375 degrees.
2. Heat the oil in a large ovenproof saucepan. Add the onions and sauté for 5 minutes. Add the chicken, pork, and sausages and brown lightly. Add the rice, stock, and salt and pepper to taste and mix well. Stir in the tomatoes, peas, and broccoli. Push the clams and mussels slightly into the rice mixture. Cover the pan with foil and bake for 45 minutes. Arrange the clams and mussels, opened and steaming, on top of the dish and serve immediately.

Green Rice Timbales

6 TO 8 SERVINGS

4 tablespoons butter or
    margarine
1 small onion, peeled and
    minced
1 cup rice
2 cups Chicken Stock, heated
    (see recipe p. 58)

Pinch of dried thyme
Salt
Freshly ground black pepper
1 cup chopped parsley

1. Preheat the oven to 375 degrees.

2. Melt the butter in an ovenproof pot. Add the onion and sauté for 5 minutes, or until it is translucent. Add the rice and cook and stir to coat the rice with the butter. Add the stock and the thyme and season with salt and pepper to taste. Bring to a boil, cover, and bake for 18 to 20 minutes. Add the parsley, using a fork to blend it into the rice.

3. Butter six or eight small molds and pack the hot rice into them. Unmold to serve.

NOTE: The rice can be molded in advance and held. Do not refrigerate, though. To reheat, put the molds into a roasting pan and pour in enough hot water to come halfway up the sides of the molds. Cover loosely with aluminum foil and bake for 30 minutes in a 350-degree oven. Unmold to serve.

Risotto Parmesan

6 SERVINGS

4 tablespoons butter or
　　margarine
1 small onion, peeled and
　　minced
1 cup rice
2 cups Chicken Stock, heated
　　(see recipe p. 58)

1 bay leaf
Salt
Freshly ground black pepper
1 cup grated Parmesan cheese

1. Preheat the oven to 375 degrees.

2. Melt the butter in an ovenproof pot. Add the onion and sauté for 5 minutes, or until it is translucent. Add the rice and cook and stir to coat the rice with the butter. Add the stock and bay leaf, season with salt and pepper to taste, and bring to a boil. Cover and bake for 18 to 20 minutes. Remove the bay leaf and use a fork to blend in the grated cheese completely.

Saffron Rice

6 SERVINGS

Pinch of saffron threads
2 cups Chicken Stock, heated
   (see recipe p. 58)
3 tablespoons butter or
   margarine

3 tablespoons finely minced
   onion
1 cup rice
Salt
Freshly ground black pepper

1. Add the saffron threads to the hot stock to dissolve them. Let them sit for 10 minutes.

2. Preheat the oven to 375 degrees.

3. Melt the butter in an ovenproof pot. Add the onion and sauté for 2 minutes. Add the rice and cook and stir to coat the rice with the butter. Add the stock with the saffron and salt and pepper to taste. Bring to a boil, cover, and bake for 18 to 20 minutes. Fluff with a fork and correct the seasonings, if necessary. This is good served with Curried Chicken (see recipe p. 110).

Sultan's Rice

6 SERVINGS

4 tablespoons butter or
   margarine
1 small onion, peeled and
   minced
1 cup rice
2 cups Chicken Stock, heated
   (see recipe p. 58)

Salt
Freshly ground black pepper
½ cup toasted almond slices
¾ cup raisins

1. Preheat the oven to 375 degrees.

2. Melt the butter in an ovenproof pot. Add the onion and sauté for 5 minutes, or until it is translucent. Add the rice and cook and stir to coat the rice with butter. Add the stock, season with salt and pepper

to taste, and bring to a boil. Cover and bake for 18 to 20 minutes. Use a fork to stir the almonds and raisins into the cooked rice. Serve immediately.

Curried Rice

6 SERVINGS

4 tablespoons butter or margarine
1 small onion, peeled and minced
1 teaspoon curry powder or to taste

1 tablespoon tomato paste
1 cup rice
2 cups Chicken Stock, heated (see recipe p. 58)
Salt
Freshly ground black pepper

1. Preheat the oven to 375 degrees.
2. Melt the butter in an ovenproof pot. Add the onion and sauté for 5 minutes, or until it is translucent. Add the curry powder and tomato paste. Stir in well and add the rice. Cook, stirring, until the rice is coated with the mixture. Add the stock, season with salt and pepper to taste, and bring to a boil. Cover and bake for 18 to 20 minutes.

Garlic Croutons

1 clove garlic, peeled and crushed
3 tablespoons butter or margarine

2 cups bread cubes from trimmed stale bread
1 tablespoon chopped parsley (optional)

Heat a heavy frying pan and, when it is hot, rub it all over with the garlic held on a fork. Discard the garlic and add the butter to the pan. When the butter has melted, add the bread cubes and toss and shake them until they are golden brown. The parsley can be tossed with the croutons after they are browned, if you like.

Potato Dumplings

6 TO 8 SERVINGS

8 potatoes, peeled
4 slices bacon, diced
1 onion, peeled and minced
2 eggs
  Pinch of dried marjoram
  Salt
  Freshly ground black pepper

  Garlic Croutons (see recipe
    p. 159), optional
5 tablespoons butter or
  margarine
½ cup bread crumbs
3 tablespoons chopped parsley

    1. Boil 4 of the potatoes in water until they are just cooked. While they are still hot, put them through a ricer or grinder.
    2. Grate the remaining potatoes into a saucepan, making sure you catch the liquid that comes from them. Cook and stir the potatoes and liquid over moderate heat until the mixture reaches the consistency of a thick cream puff dough. Cool completely.
    3. Put the bacon in a small frying pan with the onion. Sauté until the onion is soft and the bacon is barely crisp.
    4. Combine the bacon and onion, both potato doughs, and eggs. Season with marjoram and salt and pepper to taste.
    5. Shape into small balls, enclosing a crouton in the center of each ball, if desired. (It will be easier to shape the dumplings if your hands are damp. This way the dough will not stick to them.)
    6. Drop the dumplings into boiling salted water. When they rise to the surface, they are cooked. Remove them to a plate and let them drain.
    7. Melt the butter in a frying pan and add the bread crumbs. Cook and stir until the bread crumbs are brown. Add the dumplings and cook, turning them gently until they are coated with the browned bread crumbs and slightly glazed. Sprinkle with the parsley and serve immediately.

Potato Dumplings with Croutons

6 TO 8 SERVINGS

8 potatoes, peeled
Salt
Freshly ground black pepper
4 tablespoons butter or
    margarine
2 cups bread cubes, made from
    stale, trimmed bread

1 clove garlic, peeled and
    minced
3 tablespoons chopped parsley
½ cup dried bread crumbs

1. Grate the potatoes over a heavy skillet, making sure you catch all the liquid from the potatoes in the skillet. Add salt and pepper to taste and cook and stir the potatoes until the dough becomes firm but not brown. Set aside to cool.

2. Melt half the butter in a frying pan and add the bread cubes, garlic, and half the parsley. Sauté, tossing and turning, until the bread cubes are browned.

3. To form the dumplings, moisten your hand with cold water. Pinch off a piece of the potato dough and flatten it in the palm of your hand. Fill with some of the crouton mixture and roll to seal. As you finish the dumplings, put them on a piece of wax paper, making sure they do not touch.

4. Drop the dumplings into boiling salted water. When they rise to the surface, they are cooked. Remove them to a plate and let them drain.

5. Melt the remaining butter in a frying pan and add the bread crumbs and the rest of the parsley. Cook, stirring, until the bread crumbs are brown. Sprinkle over the dumplings and serve immediately.

NOTE: Another way to prepare the potato dough is to grate the potatoes, making sure you save all the liquid that comes out of them. Squeeze the potatoes dry in a towel, again saving any liquid. Then boil and reduce all the liquid and pour it over the grated potatoes and mix well.

Farina Dumplings

6 SERVINGS

2 eggs
¼ cup butter or margarine,
    melted
1 cup farina

Pinch of ground nutmeg
Salt
Freshly ground black pepper

1. Beat the eggs with the butter until foamy. Stir in the farina and season with the nutmeg and salt and pepper to taste. Let rest for approximately 5 minutes before forming the dumplings.
2. Drop the dumplings by heaping teaspoons into boiling salted water. Cook for 10 minutes. Remove from the heat and add 1 cup of cold water to the pot. Let stand for 10 minutes, drain, and serve.

Spätzle

6 SERVINGS

2 cups all-purpose flour
    Pinch of salt
4 eggs, beaten
1 cup water, or enough to make
    a thick dough

4 to 5 tablespoons butter or
    margarine

1. Mix all the ingredients except the butter in a large bowl. Use your hand to blend them well, then beat with your hand until large air bubbles form in the dough. Let the dough rest at room temperature for 10 to 15 minutes.
2. Bring a large pot of water to a boil and add salt to taste.
3. Put a small amount of the dough on a cutting board. Shave off small strips of the dough with a flat spatula. (Dip the spatula into the boiling water from time to time to prevent the dough from sticking to the spatula.)

4. Drop the spätzle into the boiling water. They are cooked when they rise to the surface. Lift them out of the pot and drain them. Refresh under cold running water and drain.

5. To serve, melt the butter in a large frying pan and add the spätzle. Toss the spätzle in the butter until they are heated through.

NOTE: The spätzle can be made up to two days in advance. Just store the drained spätzle in a covered container in the refrigerator. When you are ready to serve them, melt the butter and continue from there.

Barley Casserole

6 TO 8 SERVINGS

Salt
1½ cups pearl barley
4 tablespoons butter or
    margarine
1 onion, peeled and chopped
1 cup sliced mushrooms

Freshly ground black pepper
1½ cups Chicken, Beef, or Veal
    Stock (see recipes pp. 58,
    56, and 57)
3 tablespoons chopped parsley

1. Bring a large pot of water to a boil. Add salt to taste and the barley. Cook for 30 minutes, stirring occasionally. Drain the barley and rinse it under cold water to remove the excess starch.

2. Preheat the oven to 375 degrees.

3. Melt the butter in an ovenproof pot. Add the onion and sauté until it is soft, about 5 minutes. Add the mushrooms and sauté for 3 to 4 minutes. Season with salt and pepper to taste. Add the barley and the stock and bring to a boil on top of the stove. Cover and bake for 30 minutes, or until the barley is tender. Stir in the chopped parsley and serve.

9

Vegetables

Potatoes Duchesse, String Bean Bouquets with Pimiento and
Bacon, and Artichokes Grand Duc.

Most people don't like vegetables, except for potatoes. But
fresh vegetables can be very tasty and enjoyable if you cook them
right and do not boil the life out of them. Look through the following pages and you will see how many nice vegetable dishes you
will be able to prepare.

String Bean Bouquets

6 SERVINGS

1 pound string beans
   Salt
   Pimiento strips
   Partially cooked bacon slices
      (optional)

4 tablespoons butter or
      margarine
   Freshly ground black pepper

1. Trim the beans so that they are all the same length. Cook them in a large pot of boiling salted water until just tender, about 5 minutes. The beans should still be quite firm. Drain, refresh under cold running water, and drain again.

2. Form into equal-size bundles by tying a strip of pimiento around each bundle. Or you may tie the bundles with the partially cooked bacon.

3. Melt the butter in a frying pan and, when it is hot, add the string bean bundles and heat thoroughly. If you are using the bacon, sauté the bundles until the bacon is crisp. Season the bundles with salt and pepper to taste, and serve.

String Beans with Almonds

6 SERVINGS

1 pound string beans, trimmed
½ teaspoon dried winter savory,
      or lemon juice to taste
   Salt

3 tablespoons butter or
      margarine
   Freshly ground black pepper
⅓ cup toasted almond slices

1. Cook the beans with the savory in a large pot of boiling salted water until they are just tender, about 5 minutes. The beans should still be quite firm. Drain, refresh under cold running water, and drain again.

2. Melt the butter in a frying pan and add the string beans. Season with salt and pepper to taste. Cook and toss until hot. Sprinkle with the toasted almonds and serve at once.

Sautéed Green Beans

6 SERVINGS

1 pound string beans, trimmed
3 tablespoons butter or
   margarine
1 small onion, peeled and
   chopped

1 clove garlic, peeled and
   minced
Salt
Freshly ground black pepper

    1. Cook the string beans in a large pot of boiling salted water until they are just tender, about 5 minutes. They should still be quite firm. Drain, refresh under cold running water, and drain again.

    2. Melt the butter in a frying pan and add the onion. Sauté until the onion is golden. Add the garlic and stir it into the onion. Add the drained beans and sauté them until they are hot and well coated with the butter-and-onion mixture. Season with salt and pepper to taste.

Gratin of Broccoli

6 TO 8 SERVINGS

2 large bunches broccoli,
   trimmed
12 tablespoons butter or
   margarine
1 large onion, peeled and
   minced
1 heaping tablespoon all-
   purpose flour

3 cups milk
Salt
   Freshly ground black pepper
3 hard-cooked eggs, coarsely
   chopped
½ cup bread crumbs

    1. Parboil the broccoli in salted water. Drain well and chop coarsely.

    2. Melt 3 tablespoons of butter in a frying pan. Add the onion and sauté until soft, about 5 minutes. Add the chopped broccoli and cook and stir until all the liquid has evaporated.

3. Sprinkle the flour over the broccoli and stir in well. Add the milk a little bit at a time. Stir and wait until the liquid is absorbed before adding more milk. This should take about 15 minutes. Season the broccoli mixture with salt and pepper to taste and stir in the eggs.

4. Preheat the oven to 400 degrees.

5. Coat the inside of a gratin dish with some of the remaining butter. Pour in the broccoli mixture. Sprinkle the top with the bread crumbs and thin slices of butter cut from the remaining butter.

6. Bake for 40 minutes, or until the top is golden brown.

NOTE: The casserole may be prepared early in the day and refrigerated until ½ hour before you are going to bake it.

Artichokes Grand Duc

8 SERVINGS

1 pound fresh asparagus
Salt
1 tablespoon sugar
2 tablespoons butter or
  margarine

8 cooked artichoke bottoms
Hollandaise Sauce (see recipe
  p. 211)

1. Trim the asparagus stalks to the same length, making sure you trim off at least the white part at the bottom of each stem. Peel the stems up to the tips. Put the asparagus in a pan with salt to taste, the sugar, and the butter and cover them with water. Bring the water to a boil, cover the pan, lower the heat, and simmer for 5 to 8 minutes, or until just tender. Remove the asparagus and let them drain.

2. Preheat the oven to 350 degrees.

3. Put the cooked artichoke bottoms into a buttered baking dish. Put an equal number of asparagus spears on each artichoke bottom. Cover with Hollandaise Sauce and bake for 10 to 15 minutes, or until warmed through.

Braised Brussels Sprouts

6 SERVINGS

2 boxes fresh brussels sprouts,
    trimmed and cleaned
4 slices bacon, diced
1 onion, peeled and minced

Salt
Freshly ground black pepper
½ cup chopped parsley

1. Cook the sprouts in boiling salted water until they are barely tender. Drain, refresh under cold running water, and drain again.

2. Sauté the bacon until it is crisp. Drain off most of the grease and add the chopped onion to the pan. Sauté until the onion is golden. Add the drained sprouts and sauté until they are tender. Season with salt and pepper to taste and garnish with chopped parsley.

NOTE: To prepare the sprouts for cooking, trim the base of each one and cut a small cross into the bottom with a paring knife. This will help the stems to cook faster. If you cook the sprouts without doing this, the tops will be overcooked before the bottoms are done.

Red Cabbage

6 SERVINGS

2 tablespoons vegetable oil
½ onion, peeled and sliced
1 apple, peeled, cored, and
    sliced
1 head red cabbage, cored and
    sliced
1 potato, peeled and diced
1 tablespoon sugar

Pinch of ground cinnamon
Salt
Freshly ground black pepper
½ cup dry red wine
½ cup red wine vinegar
½ cup water
2 tablespoons duck fat or
    vegetable oil (optional)

Heat the oil in a large saucepan and add the onion and apple and sauté for 5 minutes. Add all the other ingredients and cook, covered, over low heat for 1 hour, stirring occasionally. Correct the seasonings, if necessary. Serve hot.

Sautéed Cabbage

6 SERVINGS

2 tablespoons butter, margarine,
   or oil
3 slices bacon, diced (optional)
1 large onion, peeled and diced
2 teaspoons sugar
1 head cabbage, cored, and
   sliced thin

Salt
Freshly ground black pepper
1 to 2 cups chicken broth
1 potato, peeled and grated

1. Melt the butter in a large saucepan and add the bacon and onion. Sauté until the onion is soft, about 5 minutes. Add the sugar, cabbage, and salt and pepper to taste. Stir well. Add the broth and cook, stirring often, until the cabbage is just about tender.

2. Add the grated potato and cook, stirring often, for 20 minutes, or until the mixture is thick and dry.

Sauerkraut

6 SERVINGS

2 pounds sauerkraut
2 tablespoons butter, margarine,
   or oil
2 onions, peeled and chopped
2 to 3 apples, peeled, cored, and
   chopped
2 cups dry white wine

1 bay leaf
Pinch of ground cloves
Salt
Freshly ground black pepper
6 to 8 juniper berries (optional)
1 potato, peeled and grated

1. Blanch the sauerkraut in boiling water for 5 minutes. Drain well.

2. Melt the butter in a large saucepan and add the onions and apples. Sauté until they are tender. Add the sauerkraut, wine, bay leaf, cloves, and salt and pepper to taste. Cover and cook for 1½ to 2 hours, stirring occasionally, until the tastes are well blended. Add the juniper berries, if desired, and grated potato and cook for 20 minutes longer, or until the mixture is very dry. Serve hot with sliced meats.

Julienne of Carrots and Zucchini

6 SERVINGS

4 tablespoons butter or
   margarine
1 small onion, peeled and
   minced
4 carrots, trimmed, scraped, and
   julienned

3 zucchini, trimmed and
   julienned
Salt
Freshly ground black pepper

Melt the butter in a frying pan and add the onion. Sauté until it is soft. Add the carrots and sauté for 1 or 2 minutes. Add the zucchini and sauté until the carrots and zucchini are just tender. This will take only a few minutes. Do not overcook the vegetables; they should remain crisp. Season with salt and pepper and serve immediately.

Glazed Carrots

6 SERVINGS

3 tablespoons butter or
   margarine
2 tablespoons sugar
   Pinch of salt

1 pound carrots, trimmed,
   scraped, and sliced
½ cup water

Melt the butter in a saucepan and add the sugar and salt. Stir and cook for 1 minute. Add the carrots and stir well. Add the water and cook slowly until all the liquid has evaporated and the carrots are tender and glazed.

Vichy Carrots

6 SERVINGS

3 tablespoons butter or
   margarine
1 onion, peeled and minced
1 tablespoon sugar
1 pound carrots, trimmed,
   scraped, and sliced thin

Salt
½ cup Vichy, Perrier, or regular
   water
1 tablespoon chopped parsley

Melt the butter in a saucepan and add the onion and sugar. Sauté for 3 minutes. Add the carrots, salt to taste, and the water. Cover the pot and cook over low heat for 8 to 10 minutes, or until the carrots are tender and the water has evaporated. Sprinkle with the parsley and serve at once.

Cauliflower Polonaise

6 SERVINGS

1 head cauliflower, cored
6 tablespoons butter or
   margarine

⅓ cup fine dry bread crumbs
1 hard-cooked egg, chopped
¼ cup chopped parsley

1. Cook the whole head of cauliflower in boiling salted water until it is just about tender. Drain, put in a serving bowl, and keep warm.
2. Melt the butter in a small frying pan and add the bread crumbs. Stir in the chopped egg and the parsley and cook for 1 minute. Pour over the cauliflower and serve at once.

Cauliflower in Cream Sauce

6 SERVINGS

1 head cauliflower, cored
3 tablespoons butter or
  margarine

3 tablespoons all-purpose flour
Salt
Freshly ground black pepper

1. Cook the whole head of cauliflower in boiling salted water until it is just about tender. Drain, put in a serving bowl, and keep warm. Reserve 2 cups of the cooking water and put it in a small saucepan.

2. Melt the butter in another saucepan and add the flour all at once. Stir constantly until the mixture is smooth and creamy. Remove from the heat and let the *roux* cool for a few minutes.

3. Heat the reserved cauliflower cooking liquid to the boiling point. Add it gradually to the cooled *roux*, stirring constantly. Season the sauce with salt and pepper to taste and simmer for 15 minutes, stirring occasionally. Pour the sauce over the cauliflower and serve immediately.

Corn Fritters

6 SERVINGS

3 egg yolks
1½ cups cream-style corn
½ cup all-purpose flour
Salt

Freshly ground black pepper
4 egg whites
1 cup vegetable oil

1. Beat the egg yolks until light. Add the corn, flour, and salt and pepper to taste.

2. Beat the egg whites with a pinch of salt until they are stiff. Fold them into the corn mixture.

3. Heat the oil and, when it is hot, drop the mixture into the hot oil by tablespoons. Cook until brown, turning once. Drain on paper towels and serve hot.

Ratatouille

6 SERVINGS

4 tablespoons vegetable or olive oil, or a combination of both
1 onion, peeled and sliced
2 pounds eggplant, peeled and sliced
4 zucchini, trimmed and sliced

6 tomatoes, peeled, seeded, and sliced
2 cloves garlic, peeled and minced
Salt
Freshly ground black pepper
¼ cup chopped parsley

Heat the oil in a large frying pan and add the onion. Sauté for 5 minutes, stirring occasionally. Add the eggplant, zucchini, and tomatoes. Stir in the garlic and salt and pepper to taste. Cover and simmer for 30 minutes, or until all the vegetables are tender and well blended. Sprinkle with parsley to serve. This dish may be served hot or at room temperature. Either way it is good.

Breaded Mushrooms

6 SERVINGS

2 pounds mushrooms
Flour for dredging
2 eggs, beaten with a pinch of salt

Bread crumbs for coating
3 cups vegetable oil

1. Slice the mushrooms thickly.

2. Put the flour on a piece of wax paper. Beat the eggs with the salt in a flat soup plate. Put the bread crumbs on a piece of wax paper.

3. Heat the oil. When the oil is hot, dip the mushroom pieces first into the flour, then into the egg, and finally into the bread crumbs. Use the palm of your hand to press the bread crumbs onto the mushroom slices. Drop the slices into the hot oil and fry until brown on both sides. Drain on paper towels and serve as soon as possible.

Potatoes Duchesse

6 SERVINGS

6 potatoes, peeled and cut in
    quarters
Salt
Pinch of ground nutmeg

Freshly ground black pepper
4 egg yolks, beaten
Cornstarch (optional)
1 egg, beaten

    1. Boil the potatoes in salted water until they are tender. Drain and put through a ricer while they are still hot. Add the nutmeg and salt and pepper to taste.
    2. Combine the seasoned potatoes with the beaten egg yolks and mix well. If the mixture is not thick enough to hold a shape, add some cornstarch.
    3. Preheat the oven to 400 degrees.
    4. Use a pastry bag to pipe the potatoes onto a buttered baking sheet in the shape of cones. Brush the cones with the beaten egg and bake until golden. Serve at once.

Pommes de Terre Alphonso

6 SERVINGS

6 potatoes
½ cup plus 2 tablespoons butter
    or margarine
1 tablespoon chopped parsley
1 tablespoon chopped chives

1 tablespoon chopped fresh dill
Salt
Freshly ground black pepper
½ cup grated Gruyère cheese

    1. Cook the potatoes in their jackets in boiling salted water until they are barely tender. Peel and slice the potatoes as soon as you can handle them.
    2. Preheat the oven to 400 degrees.
    3. Melt ½ cup of butter in a frying pan and add the sliced potatoes. Sprinkle on the parsley, chives, and dill and season with salt and pepper to taste. Toss the potatoes with the herbs for about 3 minutes.

4. Transfer the potatoes to a buttered baking dish. Sprinkle the grated cheese over the top and dot the top with pieces of the remaining butter. Bake for 15 to 20 minutes, or until the top is nicely browned.

Pommes Macaire

6 SERVINGS

6 potatoes, peeled, sliced, and
  cooked until tender
Pinch of ground nutmeg
Salt
Freshly ground black pepper
3 slices bacon, diced
1 onion, peeled and minced

3 egg yolks, beaten
4 tablespoons chopped parsley
3 teaspoons cornstarch
8 tablespoons butter or
  margarine
Flour for dredging

1. Put the potatoes, nutmeg, and salt and pepper to taste into the container of a blender or food processor and purée until smooth. Pour the purée into a mixing bowl and set aside.

2. Sauté the bacon and the onion together until the bacon is cooked and the onion is golden. Drain and add the bacon and onion to the potato purée with the egg yolks. Add the parsley and cornstarch and mix well. Form the mixture into wheels or rolls and cut off thick slices.

3. Melt the butter in a large frying pan. When it is hot, dredge the slices in the flour and add them to the hot butter. Sauté until golden and serve at once.

Cheese Potatoes Anna

6 SERVINGS

2 tablespoons butter or
   margarine
4 large potatoes, peeled and
   sliced
1 onion, peeled and sliced
Salt

Freshly ground black pepper
½ cup heavy cream
½ cup Chicken Stock (see recipe
   p. 58)
¼ cup grated Parmesan cheese

   1. Preheat the oven to 375 degrees.
   2. Butter a baking dish and alternate in it layers of potatoes and onions. Sprinkle the potato layers with salt and pepper. Pour the cream and stock over the vegetables and sprinkle the grated cheese over the top.
   3. Bake for 45 minutes to 1 hour, or until the potatoes are tender and the top is browned.

Pommes Boulangère

6 SERVINGS

4 slices bacon, diced
1 onion, peeled and minced
2 tablespoons butter or
   margarine
4 potatoes, peeled and sliced

Salt
Freshly ground black pepper
½ cup heavy cream
½ cup Chicken Stock (see recipe
   p. 58)

   1. Sauté the bacon and onion in a small frying pan until the onion is golden and the bacon is crisp. Drain off all grease and set aside.
   2. Preheat the oven to 375 degrees.
   3. Butter the bottom and sides of a baking dish and layer the potatoes in the dish, sprinkling each layer with salt and pepper. Pour the cream and stock over the potatoes. Spread the onion-bacon mixture in a layer on top of the potatoes.
   4. Bake for 1 hour, or until the potatoes are tender.

Snow Peas and Mushrooms

6 SERVINGS

1 tablespoon peanut or
   vegetable oil
2 scallions, cut into ¼-inch slices
1 clove garlic, peeled and
   minced
½ teaspoon grated fresh ginger

8 mushrooms, sliced thin
1 pound snow peas, strings
   removed
2 tablespoons soy sauce
1 teaspoon cornstarch, dissolved
   in 2 teaspoons water

Heat the oil in a frying pan and add the scallions, garlic, and ginger. Sauté for 1 to 2 minutes and then add the mushrooms. Cook for 1 minute. Add the snow peas and cook and stir for 3 minutes. Add the soy sauce and cook for 1 minute. Thicken the mixture with the cornstarch and water and serve immediately.

Spinach with Onions and Anchovies

6 SERVINGS

2 pounds spinach, picked over
   and washed well
3 tablespoons butter or
   margarine
1 onion, peeled and minced
3 to 4 anchovy fillets, drained

Pinch of ground nutmeg
Salt
Freshly ground black pepper
¼ cup grated Parmesan cheese
   (optional)

1. Blanch the spinach in boiling salted water. Drain, refresh under cold running water, and drain again. Squeeze out all the moisture and chop the spinach coarsely.
2. Melt the butter in a frying pan and add the onion. Sauté until the onion is soft. Add the anchovies and the spinach and sauté until the mixture is quite dry. Season with the nutmeg and salt and pepper to taste. Add the cheese, if desired, and serve immediately.

Spinach Timbales

6 SERVINGS

5 tablespoons butter or margarine
2 10-ounce packages frozen spinach leaves, thawed and drained, or 2 10-ounce packages fresh spinach, picked over and washed well

Pinch of ground nutmeg
Salt
Freshly ground black pepper
2 eggs
1 egg yolk
½ cup heavy cream
Mornay Sauce (see recipe p. 210)

1. Melt 3 tablespoons of butter in a frying pan and add the spinach. Sauté for 3 to 4 minutes. Season with the nutmeg and salt and pepper to taste. Cool and chop coarsely.

2. Preheat the oven to 375 degrees.

3. Butter six timbale molds well with the remaining butter and press an equal amount of the cooled spinach into each mold.

4. Beat the eggs, egg yolk, and heavy cream together until well combined. Pour a little of the mixture into each mold over the spinach.

5. Put the filled molds into a baking pan and pour in enough hot water to come halfway up the sides of the molds. Bake for 30 minutes, or until set and puffed. Let sit for a few minutes and turn out. Serve hot with Mornay Sauce.

Spinach Soufflé

6 SERVINGS

3 large tomatoes
  Salt
1 10-ounce package frozen
  spinach, or 1 10-ounce
  package fresh spinach,
  picked over and washed
  well

½ teaspoon minced garlic
2 egg yolks
  Freshly ground black pepper
3 tablespoons grated Parmesan
  cheese
2 egg whites

1. Cut the tomatoes in half and scoop out the seeds and pulp. Sprinkle the insides of the tomato halves with salt and turn them upside down to drain for about 20 minutes.

2. Boil the spinach until tender, drain well, and squeeze out as much liquid as possible.

3. Preheat the oven to 375 degrees.

4. Put the spinach, garlic, egg yolks, salt and pepper to taste, and 2 tablespoons of cheese in the container of a blender or food processor. Blend until puréed. Transfer to a bowl.

5. Beat the egg whites with a pinch of salt until they are stiff. Fold the beaten egg whites into the spinach purée.

6. Mound the purée into the prepared tomato shells. Put the shells in a buttered baking dish and bake for 20 minutes. Serve immediately.

Stuffed Acorn Squash

6 SERVINGS

4 acorn squash
3 tablespoons butter or
    margarine
1 small onion, peeled and
    minced
½ cup sour cream
3 tablespoons brown sugar, or to
    taste

½ teaspoon ground cinnamon
    Salt
    Freshly ground black pepper
2 tablespoons chopped parsley
1 to 1½ cups bread crumbs

1. Preheat the oven to 375 degrees.
2. Cut the squash in half and scoop out the seeds. Put the squash halves in a baking pan, cut side down, and add ½ inch hot water to the pan. Bake the squash for 50 minutes, or until the flesh is tender. Cool for a few minutes and scrape out the squash, being careful not to puncture the shells. Purée the squash flesh through a food mill or in a blender or food processor. Put into a bowl and set aside.
3. Melt the butter in a small frying pan and add the onion. Sauté until the onion is golden. Add to the puréed squash with the sour cream, brown sugar, ground cinnamon, salt and pepper to taste, and parsley. Mix well and blend in enough bread crumbs to form a firm mixture. Correct the seasonings, if necessary.
4. Spoon the stuffing into six of the acorn shells and sprinkle some bread crumbs over the stuffing. Bake in a buttered pan for 30 minutes, or until piping hot.

Spaghetti Squash

6 SERVINGS

1 3-pound spaghetti squash
    Salt

Freshly ground black pepper
Butter

1. Preheat the oven to 375 degrees.

2. Slice the squash in half and scoop out the seeds. Put the squash halves, cut side down, in a baking pan. Add about ½ inch hot water to the pan. Bake for 45 minutes to 1 hour, or until the squash is tender.

3. Remove the squash from the pan and scrape out the pulp with a fork. Put it in a serving bowl and season with salt, pepper, and butter to taste.

Tomatoes Provençale

8 SERVINGS

4 tomatoes
  Salt
  Freshly ground black pepper
1 cup bread crumbs
1 clove garlic, peeled and
    minced

3 tablespoons chopped parsley
2 tablespoons butter or
    margarine, melted

1. Preheat the oven to 375 degrees.

2. Cut the tomatoes in half and sprinkle the cut sides with salt and pepper. Put the tomatoes, cut side up, in a buttered baking dish.

3. Combine the bread crumbs, garlic, and parsley together and spread the mixture evenly over the tomato halves. Spoon the melted butter over the tops of the tomatoes.

4. Bake for 15 to 20 minutes and serve immediately.

Tomatoes Florentine

8 SERVINGS

4 tomatoes
   Salt
2 pounds fresh spinach, picked
   over and washed well
3 tablespoons butter or
   margarine

1 small onion, peeled and
   minced
3 to 4 anchovy fillets, diced
   Pinch of ground nutmeg
   Freshly ground black pepper

1. Cut the tomatoes in half and scoop out the seeds and pulp. Sprinkle the insides of the tomato halves with salt and turn them upside down to drain for about 20 minutes.
2. Blanch the spinach in boiling salted water. Drain, refresh under cold running water, and drain again. Squeeze out as much moisture as possible and chop the spinach coarsely.
3. Preheat the oven to 375 degrees.
4. Melt the butter in a frying pan and add the onion. Sauté until the onion is soft. Add the anchovies and chopped spinach. Season with nutmeg and salt and pepper to taste. Sauté until the mixture is very dry.
5. Pack the spinach into the prepared tomato shells. Put the shells into a buttered baking dish and bake for 15 minutes, or until heated through.

Baked Zucchini

8 SERVINGS

4 zucchini, washed and trimmed
   Salt
2 cloves garlic, peeled and
   crushed
   Juice of 1 lemon

½ cup vegetable or olive oil, or a
   combination of both
   Freshly ground black pepper
2 to 3 tablespoons chopped
   parsley

1. Cut the zucchini in half lengthwise and score the cut sides diagonally with a knife. Sprinkle the zucchini with salt and let them sit, cut side down, for 30 minutes.

2. Preheat the oven to 400 degrees.

3. Put the garlic in a mortar and pound it to a paste. Add the lemon juice and oil and season with salt and pepper to taste. Blend well.

4. Wipe the zucchini dry with paper towels. Put them in a buttered baking dish, cut side up. Spread the tops with equal amounts of the garlic mixture. Sprinkle the parsley evenly over the zucchini. Cover with foil and bake for 20 minutes, or until the zucchini are tender.

Zucchini Timbales

8 SERVINGS

6 medium-size zucchini,
    trimmed
Salt
3 tablespoons butter, margarine,
    or vegetable oil
1 heaping teaspoon dried
    marjoram

2 eggs
1 egg yolk
½ cup heavy cream
    Freshly ground black pepper

1. Wash the zucchini but do not peel them. Julienne them in a food processor or grate them on a large-holed hand grater. Put them into a bowl in layers, salting each layer well. Let sit for 30 minutes. Squeeze out as much moisture as possible and set the zucchini aside.

2. Melt the butter in a frying pan and add the zucchini. Sauté for a few minutes, stirring. Add the marjoram and mix in well. Set the zucchini to cool.

3. Beat the eggs, egg yolk, and cream together with pepper to taste and add the zucchini. Taste for seasonings and add salt, if necessary.

4. Preheat the oven to 400 degrees.

5. Pour the zucchini mixture into eight well-buttered timbale molds and bake for 30 minutes, or until set. Unmold and serve hot.

Sautéed Zucchini

6 SERVINGS

3 tablespoons butter or margarine
1 small onion, peeled and minced
1 clove garlic, peeled and minced

6 zucchini, trimmed and julienned
Salt
Freshly ground black pepper
2 tablespoons chopped parsley

Melt the butter in a frying pan and add the onion. Sauté for 5 minutes, stirring often. Add the garlic and zucchini. Mix well and season with salt and pepper to taste. Sauté, stirring constantly, for 2 to 3 minutes. Sprinkle with the parsley and serve.

Stir-Fried Vegetables

6 SERVINGS

4 tablespoons butter or margarine
1 cup diced onion
2 cups broccoli flowerets
2 cups cauliflower flowerets

2 yellow squash, trimmed and sliced
8 mushrooms, cut in half
Salt
4 tablespoons water

Melt the butter in a frying pan and add the onion. Sauté for 4 to 5 minutes. Then add the broccoli, cauliflower, squash, and mushrooms. Season with salt to taste and add the water. Cover the pan and cook for about 5 minutes, or until the vegetables are just crisp. Serve hot.

Turned Vegetables

6 SERVINGS

2 carrots, trimmed and scraped
2 celery stalks, trimmed
2 turnips, peeled
  Salt

Sugar
3 tablespoons butter or
  margarine
Freshly ground black pepper

1. Turn or trim each vegetable as shown on p. 7.

2. Blanch each vegetable separately in boiling water to which a pinch of salt and a pinch of sugar have been added. Drain and refresh the vegetables under cold running water. Drain again.

3. Melt the butter in a frying pan and add the drained vegetables. Sauté for a few minutes, or until they are hot through. Season with salt and pepper to taste.

10
Salads, Salad Dressings, and Relishes

Lingonberry Apples, Salad Composé, and Onion and Tomato Relish.

A good salad always adds a nice touch to a meal, so I am offering you quite a few recipes from my collection.

Also included here are some easy-to-make salad dressings and relishes that go well with meats and poultry.

Herring Salad

6 SERVINGS

1 cup chopped apple
1 cup chopped onion
½ cup diced beets
1 cup peeled, diced cooked
   potatoes
1 cup chopped Kosher dill
   pickles

1 cup diced marinated herring
   fillets
¼ cup vegetable oil
¼ cup red wine vinegar
Lettuce leaves

Mix all the salad ingredients together and then toss with the oil and vinegar. Serve on lettuce leaves.

Tuna and White Bean Salad

6 SERVINGS

1 cup dried Great Northern
   beans
½ cup minced red onion
1 7-ounce can tuna fish
   Salt
   Freshly ground black pepper
1 tablespoon red wine vinegar

2 to 3 tablespoons olive or
   vegetable oil
Lettuce leaves
1 pint cherry tomatoes,
   stemmed
Black olives

1. Pick the beans over and soak them overnight in water to cover by 2 inches. Cook until tender in water without salt. Drain and cool.

2. In a large salad bowl, mix the beans with the onion. Drain and break up the tuna and add it to the beans. Season the salad with salt and pepper to taste. Mix in the vinegar and oil.

3. Serve the salad mounded on a bed of lettuce leaves, surrounded by cherry tomatoes and black olives for garnish.

Salade Niçoise

6 SERVINGS

10 lettuce leaves
1 cup cooked green beans
2 small cucumbers, trimmed
   and diced
12 radishes, trimmed and sliced
2 7-ounce cans tuna fish,
   drained
1 red onion, peeled and sliced

1 green pepper, seeded and
   sliced
4 tomatoes, sliced
2 hard-cooked eggs, sliced
   Anchovies to taste
   French Dressing (see recipe
   p. 199)

Line a salad bowl with the lettuce leaves. Add the other ingredients, except the dressing, in layers, arranging the tomatoes, eggs, and anchovies decoratively on top. When ready to serve, pour the dressing over the salad and toss at the table.

NOTE: Usually people put potatoes in a Salade Niçoise. I don't like them with this mixture, so I don't use them.

Salade Composé

6 TO 8 SERVINGS

Tomato Salad:

¾ cup cottage or ricotta cheese
2 tablespoons yogurt
3 tablespoons vinegar
   Salt

Freshly ground black pepper
Chopped fresh parsley
Chopped fresh chives
1 pint cherry tomatoes

Put the cheese, yogurt, and vinegar into the container of a blender or food processor. Blend until very smooth. Pour into a bowl and season with salt and pepper to taste. Fold in the chopped herbs and the cherry tomatoes. Chill.

Cucumber Salad:

2 cucumbers, peeled and sliced
    thin
Salt
Vinegar

Freshly ground black pepper
Chopped fresh dill
1 tablespoon minced onion
    (optional)

Layer the cucumbers in a bowl, sprinkling each layer with salt. Let sit for 30 minutes and drain well. Mix the drained cucumbers with a little vinegar, pepper, and dill to taste. Add more salt, if necessary, and the onion, if desired.

Carrot Salad:

4 carrots, trimmed, scraped, and
    shredded
1 apple, peeled, cored, and
    shredded
Lemon juice

Salt
Freshly ground black pepper
1 to 2 tablespoons honey
    (optional)

Mix the carrots and apple with lemon juice, salt, and pepper to taste. If the salad is not sweet enough for your taste, add some honey. Cover and chill.

Endive Salad:

4 Belgian endives
1 clove garlic, peeled and
    minced
1 teaspoon Dijon mustard
2 to 3 tablespoons chopped
    parsley

Dash of ground nutmeg
Salt
Freshly ground black pepper
¼ cup red wine vinegar
¼ cup oil

1. Cut the endives in half lengthwise and cut out the core. Soak the endives in lukewarm water for 1 hour. (This will remove most of the bitterness many people complain of.) Drain the endives well and slice them.

2. Combine the garlic, mustard, parsley, nutmeg, salt and pepper to taste, vinegar, and oil. Pour over the endives and toss well.

To Assemble the Salad:

Arrange fresh spinach leaves on individual salad plates. Put equal portions of each of the salads on each of the plates and serve at once.

Pasta Salad

6 SERVINGS

1 pound pasta, such as small
   shells or elbows
½ cup broccoli flowerets
½ cup cauliflower flowerets
1 carrot, trimmed, scraped, and
   julienned
1 tomato, peeled, seeded, and
   diced

¼ cup pitted black olives
¼ cup grated Gruyère cheese
2 tablespoons finely chopped
   fresh basil, or 1 teaspoon
   dried basil
½ cup red wine vinegar
¼ cup olive oil

1. Cook the pasta in boiling salted water until it is just tender. Drain, then rinse with cold running water, and drain well.

2. Combine the cooked pasta with all the other ingredients in a large bowl. Toss together to mix completely and let the salad sit for at least 30 minutes so the flavors will blend.

Hawaiian Egg Salad

6 SERVINGS

3 slices canned pineapple,
   drained and diced
1 Kosher dill pickle, diced
2 apples, peeled, cored, and
   diced
2 whole tomatoes, cored and cut
   in wedges
½ cup mayonnaise

½ cup ketchup
1 tablespoon Worcestershire
   sauce
Salt to taste
Freshly ground black pepper
   to taste
8 hard-cooked eggs, sliced
Lettuce leaves

Combine all the ingredients except the eggs and lettuce leaves. Fold the eggs gently into the salad mixture so they don't fall apart. Serve the salad on lettuce leaves with toast or rye bread on the side.

Cottage Cheese—My Way

6 SERVINGS

3 cups cottage cheese
¾ cup diced green pepper
¾ cup chopped chives
¾ cup chopped black or green
      olives

¾ cup chopped parsley
¾ cup lemon juice
    Lettuce leaves
3 tomatoes, cored and cut in
      wedges

Combine the cottage cheese, green pepper, chives, olives, parsley, and lemon juice together in a bowl. Mix gently. Serve the salad on a bed of lettuce and garnish each serving with tomato wedges.

Artichoke and Mushroom Salad

6 SERVINGS

1 cup water
1 cup dry white wine
½ cup olive oil
    Juice of 3 lemons
1 bay leaf
    Pinch of dried thyme or dried
      oregano

Salt
Freshly ground black pepper
2 packages frozen artichoke
      hearts, thawed
2 pounds mushrooms, whole if
      they are small, quartered if
      they are large

Put the water, wine, oil, lemon juice, bay leaf, thyme, and salt and pepper to taste in a saucepan. Bring to a boil and reduce a little. Add the artichoke hearts to the marinade and cook for 5 minutes. Add the mushrooms to the marinade and cook for 3 minutes. Remove from the heat and cool the mixture. Serve at room temperature.

Avocado Salad

6 SERVINGS

½ head iceberg lettuce,
   shredded
2 large ripe avocados, peeled
   and diced

1 cup French Cocktail Sauce
   (see recipe p. 201)
12 cooked shrimp, or 6 parsley
   sprigs

1. Line six salad plates with equal portions of the shredded lettuce.

2. Mix the diced avocados with the French Cocktail Sauce and spoon the mixture over the lettuce. Top each portion with two shrimp or the parsley.

String Bean and Zucchini Salad

6 SERVINGS

2 zucchini
½ pound string beans
1 cup cauliflower flowerets
2 tablespoons minced onion
10 green olives, halved
⅓ cup red wine vinegar
1 3-ounce package cream
   cheese, softened

⅓ cup vegetable oil
½ teaspoon dried oregano
Salt
Freshly ground black pepper
Lettuce leaves

1. Trim the zucchini and cut them into 4-inch lengths. Blanch them in boiling salted water for 5 minutes, or until just barely tender. Drain and refresh under cold running water. Drain again. Set aside.

2. Cook the string beans and cauliflower in boiling salted water until *al dente*. Drain, refresh under cold running water, and drain again.

3. Cut the zucchini into large slices and put them in a bowl. Cut the string beans into 2-inch lengths and add them to the bowl with the zucchini. Add the cauliflower, onion, and olives to the bowl with the zucchini and string beans.

4. Whip the vinegar into the softened cream cheese. Mix in the oil, oregano, and salt and pepper to taste. Pour the dressing over the vegetables and mix well. Serve the salad on lettuce leaves.

Beet Salad

6 TO 8 SERVINGS

2 bunches of beets, tops removed
½ onion, peeled and sliced
1 bay leaf
½ teaspoon plus a pinch of caraway seeds

⅓ cup red wine vinegar
⅓ cup vegetable oil
Pinch of sugar
Salt
Freshly ground black pepper

1. Do not peel the beets, but wash them well. Put them in a saucepan and add the onion, bay leaf, and ½ teaspoon of caraway seeds. Add water to cover, bring to a boil, and cook until the beets are tender. Put the beets under cold running water to cool them. Peel and slice them when they are cool enough to handle. Put the sliced beets in a bowl.

2. In a small saucepan, heat the vinegar, oil, pinch of caraway seeds, sugar, and salt and pepper to taste. Pour the hot vinaigrette over the sliced beets. Cover and refrigerate until cool.

Carrot and Zucchini Salad

6 SERVINGS

3 or 4 carrots, trimmed, scraped,
  and julienned
2 small zucchini, trimmed and
  julienned
1 8-ounce container plain yogurt

2 tablespoons honey
Juice of 1 lemon
3 tablespoons chopped hazelnuts
Lettuce leaves

Put the carrots and zucchini in a bowl. Mix together the yogurt, honey, and lemon juice and pour over the vegetables. Add the nuts and toss well. Serve the salad on lettuce leaves.

Cauliflower Vinaigrette

6 SERVINGS

1 large head cauliflower, cored
½ cup chopped onion
  Pinch of sugar
  Salt

Freshly ground black pepper
Red wine vinegar
Vegetable or olive oil
2 tablespoons chopped parsley

1. Parboil the cauliflower in boiling salted water until just cooked, but still firm. Remove from the liquid and refresh under cold running water. Set aside ½ cup of the cooking liquid.
2. Separate the cauliflower into flowerets and put them in a bowl. Add the onion, sugar, salt and pepper to taste, and the reserved cooking liquid. Mix. Add vinegar and oil to taste and sprinkle the salad with chopped parsley.

Cucumber-Dill Salad

6 SERVINGS

4 cucumbers
Salt
1 cup sour cream
2 tablespoons lemon juice

Freshly ground black pepper
Chopped fresh dill
Finely minced onion (optional)

1. Peel or score the skins of the cucumbers, as you wish. Slice them thin and put the slices in a bowl, salting each layer. Let sit for at least 30 minutes. Drain off the accumulated liquid.
2. Add the sour cream, lemon juice, and pepper to taste to the cucumbers. Toss well. Add dill to taste and the onion, if desired. Taste for salt and add, if necessary.

German Cabbage Salad

6 SERVINGS

1 head green cabbage, cored and
    sliced thin
¼ pound bacon, diced
2 onions, peeled and diced
½ cup red wine vinegar

¼ cup vegetable oil
Pinch of caraway seeds
    (optional)
Salt
Freshly ground black pepper

1. Blanch the cabbage in boiling water. Drain, refresh under cold running water, and drain well.
2. Sauté the bacon and onions in a frying pan until the bacon is crisp and the onions are soft.
3. Transfer the cabbage to a bowl and pour the bacon and onions over the cabbage. Add the vinegar, oil, caraway seeds, and salt and pepper to taste. Mix well and let stand at room temperature for 2 hours to develop the flavor.

Red Cabbage Salad

6 SERVINGS

1 large head red cabbage, cored
   and sliced or shredded
1 large onion, peeled and sliced
   thin
2 apples, peeled, cored, and
   shredded

½ cup red wine vinegar
1 cup dry red wine
½ cup vegetable oil
Pinch of sugar
Pinch of ground cinnamon
Salt to taste

Combine all the ingredients together in a large bowl. Let sit at room temperature for 1 to 2 hours to develop flavor. Serve with pork or poultry.

Onions à l'Orientale

8 TO 10 SERVINGS

2 bags frozen pearl onions
1 cup raisins
½ cup water
⅓ cup vegetable oil
2 bay leaves
1 teaspoon salt
⅔ cup red wine vinegar

⅔ cup dry white wine
1 cup sugar
⅓ cup ketchup or tomato purée
1 teaspoon dried thyme
1 teaspoon freshly ground black
   pepper

Combine all the ingredients in a large saucepan. Bring to a boil, lower the heat, and simmer, uncovered, for 50 to 60 minutes. The sauce should be thick and the onions cooked through. Remove the bay leaves and correct the seasonings, if necessary. Cover and chill. Serve with pâté.

Pepper Salad

6 SERVINGS

6 large green peppers
3 tablespoons red wine vinegar
3 tablespoons olive oil
¾ teaspoon dried oregano
¾ teaspoon dried basil
2 cloves garlic, peeled and
  minced

Salt
Freshly ground black pepper
2 tablespoons dry red wine
Anchovy fillets
Tomato wedges

1. Put the green peppers into a large pot and pour boiling water over them. Let them sit for 5 to 10 minutes. Remove from the water and, when the peppers are cool enough to handle, peel them. Remove the seeds and slice the peppers into strips. Put the strips into a bowl.
2. Combine the vinegar, oil, oregano, basil, garlic, salt and pepper to taste, and wine in a small bowl. Mix well and pour over the peppers. Let sit for at least 1 hour at room temperature. Garnish the salad with anchovy fillets and tomato wedges.

German Potato Salad

6 SERVINGS

6 to 8 cooked potatoes, peeled
  and sliced
½ cup chopped onion
1 to 2 teaspoons chopped
  parsley
¼ cup red wine vinegar

¼ cup vegetable oil
Pinch of salt
Pinch of black pepper
½ cup warm Chicken Stock (see
  recipe p. 58)

Mix all the ingredients in a bowl, tossing to combine well.

Spinach Salad

6 SERVINGS

2 cups julienned spinach leaves
2 cups julienned peeled apples
2 cups julienned mushrooms
6 tablespoons orange juice

6 tablespoons honey
6 tablespoons ground toasted
   hazelnuts

Combine all the ingredients in a salad bowl and toss well. Serve immediately.

Tomato and Cucumber Salad

6 SERVINGS

4 cucumbers
   Salt
4 tomatoes, cored and cut into
   wedges
1 cup sour cream

2 tablespoons lemon juice
   Freshly ground black pepper
4 tablespoons chopped parsley
4 tablespoons minced onion
   (optional)

Peel or score the skins of the cucumbers, as you wish. Slice them thin and layer the slices in a bowl, salting each layer. Let sit for at least 30 minutes. Drain well. Add the tomato wedges, sour cream, lemon juice, pepper to taste, and salt, if needed. Stir in the chopped parsley and the onion, if desired. Cover and chill until ready to serve.

Yogurt Salad

6 SERVINGS

3 cucumbers, peeled, seeded,
   and diced
3 tomatoes, peeled, seeded, and
   diced
1 large onion, peeled and diced

Salt to taste
Freshly ground black pepper
   to taste
Juice of ½ lemon
1 cup plain yogurt

Put all the ingredients in a bowl, toss, and serve.

French Dressing

⅓ cup red wine vinegar
⅓ cup vegetable oil
⅓ cup water
   Pinch of sugar

Salt to taste
Freshly ground black pepper
   to taste

Put all the ingredients into a jar with a close-fitting lid. Shake to combine completely and let stand for 1 hour to develop the flavor. Add to the salad at serving time and toss.

Russian Dressing

1 recipe French Dressing (see
   p. 199)

1 hard-cooked egg, diced
1 tablespoon minced onion

Combine the ingredients well and add to the salad at serving time.

Mayonnaise

1 egg
1 tablespoon red wine vinegar
Pinch of paprika
1 teaspoon Dijon mustard
Salt
Freshly ground black pepper
1½ cups vegetable oil

Put the egg, vinegar, paprika, mustard, and salt and pepper to taste into the container of a food processor. Blend for a few seconds. With the motor running, add the oil very, very slowly, until the mixture is of the proper consistency. The mayonnaise may be stored in a covered jar in the refrigerator for a week or two.

Sauce Ravigote

1 cup Mayonnaise (see above)
1 tablespoon cooking liquid from spinach or from chopped parsley
1 teaspoon chopped fresh tarragon
1 teaspoon chopped parsley
1 teaspoon chopped watercress

Mix the cooking liquid with the Mayonnaise and fold in the chopped herbs. Serve with poached eggs or cold fish dishes.

Sauce Tartare

1 cup Mayonnaise (see above)
1 tablespoon chopped parsley or chives
1 tablespoon minced onion
1 hard-cooked egg, chopped
1 tablespoon chopped pickles
Salt
Freshly ground black pepper

Mix the Mayonnaise, parsley, onion, egg, and pickles together. Season with salt and pepper to taste.

Rémoulade Sauce

1 cup Mayonnaise (see recipe
   p. 200)
2 tablespoons minced pickles
1 tablespoon drained minced
   capers
2 tablespoons minced onion
1 hard-cooked egg, minced
2 tablespoons minced parsley

Vinegar to taste
2 tablespoons pickle juice
Pinch of dried tarragon
Few drops of Worcestershire
   sauce
Salt to taste
Freshly ground black pepper
   to taste

Mix all the ingredients together, cover, and chill. Serve with fish mousse.

Sauce Andalouse

1 cup Mayonnaise (see recipe
   p. 200)
2 tablespoons tomato
   purée

½ red pepper, peeled and
   julienned
½ green pepper, peeled and
   julienned

Mix all the ingredients together and chill well. Serve with cold chicken or fish.

French Cocktail Sauce

1 cup Mayonnaise (see recipe
   p. 200)
1 tablespoon horseradish
¼ cup ketchup
   Juice of ½ lemon
   Few drops of Worcestershire
   sauce

1 to 2 tablespoons brandy
Salt to taste
Freshly ground black pepper
   to taste
½ cup heavy cream, whipped

Mix all the ingredients, except the cream, together and chill. At serving time, fold in the whipped cream and serve.

Cranberry-Orange Relish

2 oranges
2 cups cranberries
½ cup sugar

1 to 2 tablespoons kirsch
¼ cup toasted almond slices

Peel the oranges completely, making sure you remove all the pith. Cut the oranges into quarters and remove the seeds. Put the oranges and cranberries into the container of a food processor or blender. Grind until they are coarsely chopped. Remove to a bowl and stir in the remaining ingredients. Chill well.

Onion and Tomato Relish

1 cup diced onion
2 cups diced tomatoes
¼ cup chopped parsley
¼ cup red wine vinegar
¼ cup vegetable oil

Salt to taste
Freshly ground black pepper
  to taste
4 fresh basil leaves, chopped
  (optional)

Mix all the ingredients together and let stand for at least ½ hour to develop the flavor.

Lingonberry Apples

6 SERVINGS

3 apples   Sugar
1 can lingonberries, drained   Dry white wine

　　1. Preheat the oven to 375 degrees.
　　2. Peel and core the apples and cut them in thick slices. Put them in a baking dish and fill the centers with the lingonberries. Sprinkle with sugar and pour white wine halfway up the apple slices.
　　3. Bake for about 15 minutes, or until tender. Serve with roast goose.

Sautéed Apple Slices

6 SERVINGS

2 to 3 apples, peeled and cored   3 tablespoons butter
　Juice of ½ lemon   5 tablespoons sugar

　　1. Cut the apples into wedges about ½ inch thick. Sprinkle them with the lemon juice.
　　2. Melt the butter and add the sugar. Cook for 1 or 2 minutes and add the apple slices. Sauté them until they are golden on the outside and cooked through. Serve with Curried Chicken (see recipe p. 110).

Fried Bananas

6 SERVINGS

3 large bananas
   Flour for dredging
2 eggs

Bread crumbs for coating
6 tablespoons butter or
   margarine

1. Peel and slice the bananas in half lengthwise. Slice again crosswise.

2. Put the flour on a piece of wax paper. Beat the eggs in a flat soup plate until they are well combined. Put the bread crumbs on a piece of wax paper.

3. Melt the butter in a large frying pan and, when it begins to sizzle, dredge the banana pieces in the flour, dip them in the beaten eggs, then coat them with the bread crumbs. Press down lightly with the palm of your hand to help the crumbs stick to the banana slices. Drop the coated bananas into the hot butter and sauté until they are golden brown, turning once. Serve immediately. Fried bananas are excellent with curry dishes.

Goulash Spice

   Peel of 1 lemon (yellow part
     only)
3 cloves garlic, peeled
1 bay leaf

1 teaspoon salt
½ teaspoon caraway seeds
   Pinch of dried thyme
   Pinch of dried oregano

Put all the ingredients on a chopping board and mince as finely as possible with a large sharp knife. Store in a tightly closed jar in the refrigerator.

11

Sauces and Butters

Tomato Sauce, Soubise Sauce, Butter Garnish, Horseradish Cream, and Garlic Paste.

Sauce Demi-Glace

8 tablespoons vegetable oil
2 pounds veal or pork bones
2 carrots, trimmed and
   chopped
2 unpeeled onions, chopped
3 celery stalks, trimmed and
   chopped
2 cloves garlic, peeled

5 tomatoes, diced, or 1 large can
   whole tomatoes, or ½ cup
   tomato paste
1 bay leaf
4 parsley sprigs
  Salt
  Freshly ground black pepper
6 tablespoons all-purpose flour

1. Preheat the oven to 400 degrees.

2. Put 2 tablespoons of oil in a large roasting pan, add the bones, and roast until the bones are browned.

3. Add the carrots, onions, celery, garlic, and tomatoes and roast for 30 minutes longer.

4. Deglaze the pan by adding ½ cup water to the pan every 10 minutes. Stir the water in well, reaching all over the bottom and up on the sides of the pan with your wooden spoon. Add ½ cup water to the pan five or six times more, stirring the water in well each time.

5. Pour and scrape all the ingredients from the roasting pan into a large stockpot. Add the bay leaf, parsley sprigs, and salt and pepper to taste. Pour in about 12 cups water. Bring to a boil, lower the heat, and simmer for about 6 hours. Strain the stock into a clean bowl and discard the bones and vegetables.

6. Melt the remaining 6 tablespoons oil in a pot large enough to hold the strained stock. Add the flour all at once and stir until the mixture is thick and creamy. Cool. Gradually add the hot strained stock to the cooled *roux* and cook and stir until the floury taste is gone. Chill the stock and remove the layer of fat which will have risen to the top. The stock can now be refrigerated or frozen.

Brown Sauce or Espagnole

2 tablespoons vegetable oil
2 pounds beef, veal, or pork
   bones
2 carrots, trimmed and chopped
2 onions, peeled and chopped
2 celery stalks, trimmed and
   chopped
4 tomatoes, cored and chopped
2 cloves garlic, peeled

1 bay leaf
4 parsley sprigs
   Pinch of dried thyme
   Salt
   Freshly ground black pepper
6 tablespoons butter or
   margarine
6 tablespoons all-purpose flour

1. Preheat the oven to 400 degrees.

2. Put the oil in a large roasting pan, add the bones, and roast until the bones are browned well.

3. Add the carrots, onions, celery, tomatoes, and garlic and continue to brown for about 1 hour. Deglaze the pan occasionally by adding some water to it and stirring the water in well.

4. Pour and scrape all the ingredients from the roasting pan into a large stockpot. Add the bay leaf, parsley, thyme, and salt and pepper to taste. Pour in about 16 cups of water. Bring to a boil, lower the heat, and simmer for 5 to 6 hours. Strain the stock into a clean bowl and discard the bones and vegetables.

5. Melt the butter in a pot large enough to hold the strained stock. Add the flour all at once and stir until the mixture is thick and creamy. Cool. Gradually add the hot strained stock to the cooled *roux* and cook and stir until the floury taste is gone. Chill the stock and remove the layer of fat that will have risen to the top. The stock can now be used as a base for meat sauces.

Sauce Chasseur

2 tablespoons butter or
    margarine
½ cup chopped onion
½ cup chopped mushrooms

2 cups Brown Sauce (see recipe
    p. 207)
1 tablespoon chopped parsley

Melt the butter in a saucepan and add the onion. Sauté until the onion is translucent. Add the mushrooms and sauté for 5 minutes. Add the Brown Sauce and cook for 5 minutes longer. Add the chopped parsley just before serving. Serve with pork, game, or fowl.

Truffle Sauce

1 cup sliced mushrooms
½ cup Madeira
½ cup Bordeaux
2 cups Brown Sauce (see recipe
    p. 207)

Chopped truffles and their
    juice

Chop the mushrooms finely in a blender or food processor. Put the mushrooms in a saucepan with the wines. Reduce the liquid by half over medium-high heat. Add the Brown Sauce and cook for 5 minutes. Add the truffles with their juice and heat through. Serve with beef.

NOTE: When using this sauce with veal, add cream to taste.

Sauce Robert

½ cup chopped shallots
1 cup plus 1 tablespoon dry
    white wine

2 cups Brown Sauce (see recipe
    p. 207)
2 tablespoons Dijon mustard

Put the shallots and 1 cup of wine into a saucepan. Cook over medium-high heat until the liquid is reduced by half. Add the Brown Sauce and heat for 1 or 2 minutes. Mix the mustard with 1 tablespoon of wine until it forms a paste. Whisk this into the sauce and heat through. Serve with pork.

Tarragon Cream Sauce

2 tablespoons butter or
    margarine
2 shallots, peeled and minced
½ cup dry white wine
½ cup Chicken Stock (see recipe
    p. 58)

1 teaspoon tarragon vinegar
2 tablespoons chopped fresh
    tarragon
½ cup heavy cream
  Salt
  Freshly ground black pepper

Melt the butter in a saucepan. Add the shallots and sauté for 3 to 4 minutes. Add the wine and reduce by half. Add the stock, vinegar, and fresh tarragon and reduce a little. Stir in the cream and season with salt and pepper to taste. Cook over low heat to reduce slightly.

Béchamel Sauce

4 tablespoons butter or
    margarine
4 tablespoons all-purpose flour
1 cup milk

1 cup Chicken Stock (see recipe
    p. 58)
  Salt
  Freshly ground black pepper

Melt the butter in a saucepan and add the flour all at once, stirring until the mixture is smooth and creamy. Remove from the heat and cool. Heat the milk and stock together and add gradually to the cooled *roux*. Return to the heat and cook slowly for about 15 minutes, or until the floury taste is gone. Season the sauce with salt and pepper to taste.

Mornay Sauce

2 cups Béchamel Sauce (see
    recipe p. 209)
1 cup grated Swiss or Parmesan
    cheese

2 egg yolks plus an equal
    amount of heavy cream
Salt
Freshly ground black pepper

    Heat the Béchamel Sauce and add the cheese. Stir to melt the cheese. Taste and correct the seasonings, if necessary. Beat the egg yolks and cream together and add to the sauce, stirring with a whisk. Heat gently for 1 minute but do not boil the sauce.

Soubise Sauce

6 tablespoons butter or
    margarine
1 pound onions, peeled and
    chopped
¼ cup raw rice
1 cup Chicken Stock (see recipe
    p. 58)

Pinch of ground nutmeg
Salt
Freshly ground black pepper
¼ cup heavy cream

    1. Preheat the oven to 375 degrees.

    2. Melt the butter in an ovenproof pot. Add the onions and sauté until the onions are translucent. Add the rice and stir well to coat the rice with the butter. Add the stock, the nutmeg, and salt and pepper to taste. Cover and bake for 40 minutes, or until the rice is very tender. (Add a little more stock if the rice dries out too much.) Remove from the oven and let cool a little.

    3. Put the cooled onion-rice mixture into the container of a blender or food processor with the cream. Blend until smooth.

Hollandaise Sauce

6 egg yolks
½ cup dry white wine
12 ounces clarified butter (see
    below)

Salt
Freshly ground black pepper

1. Put the egg yolks and wine into a heavy saucepan. Beat together over medium heat until they are thickened.

2. Remove from the heat and continue to beat until the mixture cools a little.

3. Beat in the clarified butter with a wire whisk, beating until the ingredients are well combined. Season with salt and pepper to taste. Do not reheat the sauce. If you have to keep it warm, place it over a pot of hot water.

NOTE: If you are hesitant about putting the saucepan directly over the heat, you can combine the egg yolks and wine in the top of a double boiler over gently boiling water. Remember, too, that the egg yolk mixture and the clarified butter should be at about the same temperature (140 degrees) to combine properly.

Clarified Butter

Put 1 pound of unsalted butter in a small saucepan and melt it over high heat. As it bubbles, a foam will come to the surface. When this foam subsides and sinks to the bottom of the pan the butter will be clarified. Pour off the clear portion of butter on the top. This is your clarified butter.

Sauce Béarnaise

½ cup dry white wine
2 shallots, peeled and chopped
6 to 10 peppercorns, crushed
¼ cup tarragon vinegar
1 to 2 teaspoons dried tarragon

2 cups Hollandaise Sauce (see
   recipe p. 211)
1 teaspoon chopped parsley
1 teaspoon chopped fresh
   tarragon

Put the wine, shallots, peppercorns, vinegar, and dried tarragon into a small saucepan. Reduce over medium-high heat until there is only 1 tablespoon of liquid left. Strain well, pressing the shallots and peppercorns with the back of a spoon to extract all the moisture. Add the liquid to the Hollandaise Sauce with the parsley and fresh tarragon.

Sauce Choron

2 shallots, peeled and chopped
¼ cup tarragon vinegar
½ cup dry white wine
6 to 10 peppercorns, crushed

2 tablespoons tomato purée
2 cups Hollandaise Sauce (see
   recipe p. 211)

Put the shallots, vinegar, wine, peppercorns, and purée into a small saucepan. Reduce over medium-high heat until there is only 1 tablespoon of liquid left. Strain well and add the liquid to the Hollandaise Sauce. Serve with fish and egg dishes.

Sauce Mousseline

½ to ¾ cup heavy cream

2 cups Hollandaise Sauce (see
   recipe p. 211)

Whip the cream until it is stiff. Combine carefully with the Hollandaise Sauce. Serve immediately. This is very good with fresh asparagus.

Velouté or White Wine Fish Sauce

6 tablespoons butter or margarine
½ cup all-purpose flour

4 cups Fish Stock (see recipe p. 58)

Melt the butter in a small heavy saucepan. Add as much flour as the butter will absorb. Add the stock to the base gradually, stirring until it is well combined. Cook for about 15 minutes, or until the floury taste is gone. This sauce can be used as a base for fish sauces.

Sauce Badenia

½ cup julienned carrots
½ cup julienned celery
½ cup dry white wine
4 cups Velouté (see recipe p. 213)

2 tablespoons chopped fresh dill, or 1 teaspoon dried dill
3 egg yolks plus an equal amount of heavy cream

1. Cook the vegetables in boiling salted water until they are just tender. Drain, refresh under cold running water, and drain well.
2. Combine the wine and Velouté in a saucepan and heat, stirring. Add the vegetables and the dill.
3. Beat the egg yolks and cream together and add to the sauce, stirring. Heat gently for 1 minute but do not boil the sauce.

Sauce Doria

4 cups Velouté (see recipe
   p. 213)
1 cup diced unpeeled
   cucumbers

½ to 1 cup Champagne
3 egg yolks plus an equal
   amount of heavy cream

Combine the Velouté with the cucumber. Add the Champagne and heat gently. Beat the egg yolks and cream together and add to the sauce, stirring. Heat gently but do not boil the sauce.

Sauce Alsacienne

¼ cup julienned leeks
¼ cup julienned carrots
½ cup butter or margarine
½ cup all-purpose flour
2½ cups Fish Stock, heated (see
   recipe p. 58)

2 egg yolks
½ cup heavy cream
2 tablespoons finely chopped
   fresh dill

1. Poach the leeks and carrots in boiling salted water until tender. Drain, refresh under cold running water, and drain well.

2. Melt the butter in a saucepan and add the flour all at once. Cook for 1 or 2 minutes and gradually pour in the heated stock, stirring to combine well. Cook for a few minutes until the floury taste is gone. Add the drained leeks and carrots to the sauce.

3. Beat the egg yolks and cream together and add to the sauce, stirring. Add the dill and heat the sauce gently but do not boil. Serve immediately. This sauce goes well with poached or broiled fish.

Cumberland Sauce

3 oranges
1½ lemons
1 cup orange juice
½ cup lemon juice

1½ cups Burgundy
Pinch of cayenne
¼ cup dry mustard
1½ cups currant jelly

1. Peel the oranges and lemons, being careful not to remove the pith with the peel. Julienne the orange and lemon peels.

2. Put the julienned peels into a saucepan with the orange juice, lemon juice, Burgundy, cayenne, and mustard. Cook slowly until reduced by half.

3. Add the currant jelly, bring to a boil, and cook for 15 to 20 minutes. Serve cold with pâtés and terrines.

Curry Sauce

3 tablespoons vegetable oil
1 onion, peeled and minced
1 apple, peeled, cored, and
   chopped fine
½ cup all-purpose flour
3 cups Chicken or Beef Stock
   (see recipes pp. 58 and 56)

2 teaspoons curry powder
Salt
Freshly ground black pepper
½ cup heavy cream

1. Heat the oil in a saucepan and add the onion and apple. Sauté until they are light brown. Sprinkle the flour over the apple and onion and mix in well. Cook for a few minutes, remove from the heat, and cool.

3. Add the curry powder to the cooled *roux* and immediately add the heated stock, pouring it in slowly while stirring constantly. Season the sauce with salt and pepper to taste. Simmer for 30 minutes.

4. Strain the sauce into a clean saucepan and discard the onion and apple. Add the cream to the sauce and correct the seasonings, if necessary. Heat the sauce a little but do not boil.

Horseradish Sauce

4 tablespoons butter or
    margarine
4 tablespoons all-purpose flour
1½ cups Beef Stock (see recipe
    p. 56)
1½ cups milk

2 to 3 tablespoons drained
    grated horseradish
Juice of ½ lemon
Sugar
Salt
Freshly ground black pepper

1. Melt the butter in a saucepan and add the flour all at once, stirring until the mixture is smooth and creamy. Cook, stirring, for a few minutes. Remove from the heat and let the *roux* cool.

2. Combine the stock and milk and bring the liquid just to a boil. Off the burner, add to the cooled *roux*, stirring constantly until well combined. Return to the heat and cook for 20 minutes, or until the floury taste is gone. Add the horseradish, lemon juice, and sugar, salt, and pepper to taste. Serve with boiled beef.

Horseradish Cream

2 tablespoons drained grated
    horseradish
½ cup heavy cream, whipped
    stiff

Juice of ½ lemon

Combine all ingredients gently. Serve with poached fish.

Mustard Sauce

½ cup Dijon mustard
2 tablespoons dry mustard
4 tablespoons sugar
3 tablespoons vinegar

1 cup vegetable oil
3 tablespoons chopped fresh dill
3 tablespoons chopped parsley
1 hard-cooked egg, chopped

Mix the mustard, mustard powder, sugar, and vinegar together. Gradually beat in the oil. Fold in the herbs and egg. Serve with poached eggs.

Tomato Sauce

3 tablespoons vegetable or olive oil
1 onion, peeled and chopped
1 celery stalk, trimmed and chopped
1 small carrot, trimmed, scraped, and chopped
1 clove garlic, peeled and crushed

1 large can Italian plum tomatoes
Pinch of dried basil
Pinch of dried oregano
Salt
Freshly ground black pepper

1. Heat the oil in a saucepan and add the onion, celery, and carrot. Sauté for about 5 minutes. Add the garlic and tomatoes and mix well. Season with basil, oregano, and salt and pepper to taste. Cook for 30 minutes.
2. Purée the sauce through a food mill. Correct the seasonings, if necessary, and serve hot with Fritto Misto (see recipe p. 139).

Beurre Blanc

3 tablespoons chopped shallots
¼ cup white wine vinegar
¼ cup dry white wine

Salt to taste
1 cup butter or margarine

Combine the shallots, vinegar, wine, and salt in a small saucepan. Bring to a boil and reduce until the liquid has almost all evaporated. Cool a little. Put the pan back over very low heat and whisk in the butter very slowly, bit by bit. Keep warm over a pan of hot water, if necessary. Do not reheat the sauce.

Butter Garnish

½ cup diced onion
½ cup dry red wine
1 pound butter or margarine,
   softened

Pinch of salt
Juice of 1 lemon

1. Cook the onion and red wine together until the liquid has evaporated and the onion has turned red.

2. Put the butter in a mixing bowl and add the onion, salt, and lemon juice. Beat for 10 to 15 minutes.

3. Form the butter mixture into rolls. Wrap in parchment paper and refrigerate or freeze. Sliced into rounds, this is a good garnish for fish or chicken.

Herb Butter

1 pound butter or margarine,
   softened
2 tablespoons chopped parsley
1 to 2 cloves garlic, peeled and
   crushed

1 teaspoon salt
½ teaspoon pepper
Juice of ½ lemon

Beat all the ingredients together until very well combined. This can be refrigerated in a tightly covered jar for up to 3 weeks, or it can be frozen. Use when you are sautéing, or spread on bread and toast or heat in the oven.

Mustard Butter

¼ cup butter or margarine
   Juice of ½ lemon
½ tablespoon minced parsley
1 tablespoon minced onion
1 small clove garlic, peeled and
   minced

¼ teaspoon dry mustard
   Salt to taste
   Freshly ground black pepper
   to taste

Melt the butter and add all the other ingredients. Cook together for 1 or 2 minutes. Correct the seasonings, if necessary. Serve with fish.

Snail Butter

1 pound butter or margarine,
   softened
2 tablespoons chopped parsley
1 to 2 cloves garlic, peeled and
   crushed

   Juice of ½ lemon
   Dash of Pernod
1 teaspoon salt
½ teaspoon pepper

Beat all the ingredients together until very well combined. Form the butter mixture into rolls and wrap in parchment paper. Refrigerate or freeze, cutting off a slice at a time as needed. Serve with broiled meats.

Garlic Paste

Put 1 or 2 teaspoons of salt and 1 or 2 peeled garlic cloves on a chopping board. Using a broad chef's knife, chop the garlic fine, then turn the knife on its side and mash the garlic into the salt with the flat of the blade. It should take only a few minutes to form a fine paste. This can be used whenever a recipe calls for crushed garlic. Just remember to reduce the salt in the recipe because the garlic paste already has salt.

Garlic Oil

1 cup vegetable oil   6 to 7 cloves garlic, peeled

Combine the oil and garlic cloves in a jar with a tight-fitting lid. Let them blend for 2 days. You will then have garlic-flavored oil to use in those dishes that call for minced garlic. Garlic oil will keep for 1 to 2 months in the refrigerator.

12

Reruns

Rice Salad and Beef with Mustard and Onions.

I'm sure there have been days when you've looked in your refrigerator and found it filled with little bowls of leftover vegetables and plates of cold chicken and meat. Of course, there's never enough for another complete meal. So what do you do? As you don't want to throw the food out, because that's wasteful, let me give you some ways to use those leftovers so no one will ever know they are eating leftovers.

Vegetable Omelet

2 tablespoons butter or
    margarine for each
    omelet
3 beaten eggs for each
    omelet

1 cup diced cooked vegetables
    (such as carrots, potatoes,
    cauliflower, broccoli) for
    each omelet
Cracked black pepper

Melt the butter in a frying pan and, when it is hot, add the eggs. Sprinkle the vegetables on top of the eggs and cook over very low heat until the eggs are done to your preference. Sprinkle with cracked black pepper and serve open-faced.

Sformati di Verdura

6 SERVINGS

6 tablespoons butter or
    margarine
½ cup all-purpose flour
2 cups milk
4 egg yolks, beaten
2 cups firm-cooked vegetables

3 tablespoons grated Parmesan
    or Romano cheese
Pinch of ground nutmeg
Salt
Freshly ground black pepper
Bread crumbs

1. Melt the butter in a saucepan and add the flour all at once, stirring until the mixture is smooth and creamy. Remove from the heat and cool a little.

2. Bring the milk just to the boiling point and add it slowly to the cooled *roux*, stirring until the mixture is smooth and well combined. Cook for 15 to 20 minutes, or until the floury taste is gone. Cool.

3. Combine the cooled cream sauce with the egg yolks, vegetables, and cheese. Season with the nutmeg and salt and pepper to taste.

4. Preheat the oven to 400 degrees.

5. Butter a loaf pan well and coat it all over the inside with bread crumbs. Shake out any excess bread crumbs and pour the vegetable mixture into the pan. Put the pan in a roasting pan and pour in enough hot water to come halfway up the sides of the loaf pan. Bake for 1 hour, or until set. If the top is browning too much, cover it with foil. Remove from the oven and let rest for 15 to 20 minutes. Unmold and slice to serve.

NOTE: You can use any vegetable or combination of vegetables for this dish. Just be sure that they are not overcooked, because they are going to cook again.

Viennese Breaded Beef

6 SERVINGS

Dijon mustard
6 thin slices roast beef or pot
    roast
Flour for dredging
1 egg, beaten in a flat soup
    plate

Bread crumbs
4 tablespoons butter or
    margarine

Spread a thin coating of mustard on one side of each slice of beef. Dredge the slices in the flour, then dip them into the egg, and finally coat them with the bread crumbs, pressing the crumbs on with the palm of your hand. Sauté the coated beef in the butter for 1 or 2 minutes a side, or until nicely browned.

Beef with Mustard and Onions

6 SERVINGS

6 slices cooked beef
  Salt
  Freshly ground black pepper
6 teaspoons Dijon mustard

1½ cups chopped onions
1½ cups all-purpose flour
6 to 8 tablespoons vegetable oil

1. Pound the beef slices and season them with salt and pepper. Spread a thin layer of mustard on one side of the slices. Cover the mustard with onions and press the onions down with the palm of your hand. (Make sure you distribute the onions evenly on the slices.)
2. Coat the beef with the flour, pressing it in with the palm of your hand.
3. Heat the oil in a large frying pan and add the beef slices, onion-covered side down. Brown well and turn carefully with a spatula and brown on the other side.

Meat Loaf Leftover

6 SERVINGS

4 tablespoons butter or
   margarine
1 medium-size onion, peeled
   and sliced thin
1 large red pepper, seeded and
   sliced thin

1 dill pickle, sliced thin
½ cup dry red wine
6 slices meat loaf, heated

Melt the butter in a large frying pan and add the onion. Sauté for about 5 minutes, breaking the slices into rings. Add the pepper and sauté for 5 minutes longer. Add the dill pickle and sauté for 1 minute. Pour the wine into the pan and stir with a wooden spoon to incorporate any browned-on bits into the sauce. Cook for 1 minute. Pour the sauce over the meat loaf slices and serve at once.

Swiss Noodle Dish

2 SERVINGS

2 tablespoons butter or
   margarine
1 cup diced ham
1 cup cooked noodles, cut into
   small pieces

½ cup diced Swiss cheese
3 eggs, beaten
   Salt
   Freshly ground black pepper

Melt the butter in a frying pan and add the ham and noodles. Sauté for 1 to 2 minutes to heat through. Add the cheese and push all the ingredients to the side of the pan opposite the handle. Pour the eggs into the empty part of the pan. Rotate the pan with a circular motion over the heat so that all the ingredients are combined. Cook over low heat until the eggs are done to your preference. Fold the omelet over and turn out onto a serving plate.

Lamb "Gascone"

6 SERVINGS

2 tablespoons butter or
   margarine
2 cloves garlic, peeled and
   minced
½ cup chopped onion
½ cup chopped carrots
2 tablespoons all-purpose flour
1 cup Chicken Stock (see recipe
   p. 58)

Salt
Freshly ground black pepper
1 cup peeled, diced potatoes
2 cups cubed cooked lamb
1 tablespoon chopped fresh
   savory, or 1 teaspoon dried
   savory
2 tablespoons chopped parsley

1. Melt the butter in a saucepan and add the garlic, onion, and carrots. Sauté for 5 minutes, stirring often. Sprinkle the flour over the vegetables and stir to combine. Remove from the heat and let cool.

2. Heat the stock just to the boiling point and add it slowly to the cooled vegetable mixture, stirring constantly. Season with salt and pepper to taste. Bring the sauce to a boil, stirring constantly. Add the potatoes, lower the heat to simmer, and cook until the potatoes are just tender.

3. Add the lamb, savory, and parsley and cook gently until the potatoes are tender.

NOTE: Turnips can be substituted for the carrots. This dish can be served with noodles instead of potatoes.

Chicken Pomidoro

6 SERVINGS

4 tablespoons butter or
    margarine
2½ to 3 cups diced cooked
    chicken
1 large tomato, peeled, seeded,
    and diced
¼ cup minced onion

Salt
Freshly ground black pepper
¼ cup heavy cream or dry
    white wine
Pinch of dried basil
1 tablespoon chopped parsley

Melt the butter and add the chicken. Cook for 1 minute to heat through. Remove the chicken to a plate and add the tomato and onion to the frying pan. Sauté for 2 minutes and season with salt and pepper to taste. Add the cream, basil, and parsley and stir. Return the chicken to the pan and cook for 2 minutes longer.

Chicken Curry Dinner

6 SERVINGS

3 tablespoons butter or
    margarine
3 cups diced chicken
6 slices drained canned
    pineapple, diced
2 teaspoons curry powder

Salt
Freshly ground black pepper
1½ cups dry white wine
¾ cup heavy cream
6 drained canned figs
½ cup toasted almond slices

Melt the butter in a saucepan and add the chicken cubes, pineapple, curry powder, and salt and pepper to taste. Stir to combine. Add the wine and cook to reduce the liquid a little. Stir in the cream and heat through but do not boil. Serve over rice, garnished with the figs and almonds.

Turkey Florentine

6 SERVINGS

2 10-ounce packages fresh
  spinach, picked over
3 tablespoons butter or
  margarine

Pinch of ground nutmeg
6 slices white-meat turkey
3 tablespoons grated Parmesan
  cheese

1. Blanch the spinach in boiling salted water. Drain and squeeze out as much of the moisture as possible. Chop the spinach.
2. Melt the butter in a frying pan and add the spinach and nutmeg. Sauté until the spinach is quite dry.
3. Preheat the oven to 375 degrees.
4. Spread the spinach in the bottom of a gratin dish. Top with the turkey slices. Sprinkle the cheese over the turkey and bake for 15 to 20 minutes, or until heated through.

Turkey with Curry Sauce

6 SERVINGS

3 cups cooked Rice Pilaf (see
  recipe p. 155)
6 slices white-meat turkey

2 cups Curry Sauce (see recipe
  p. 215)

Butter a casserole and spread the Rice Pilaf in the bottom of the dish. Top with the turkey slices. Pour the Curry Sauce over the turkey and bake in a 350-degree oven for 15 to 20 minutes, or until heated through.

Salmon Mousse

6 SERVINGS

2 cups leftover salmon, flaked
2 cups Velouté (see recipe
    p. 213)
Juice of 1 lemon

4 tablespoons unflavored gelatin
Salt
Freshly ground black pepper
6 egg whites

1. Mix the fish with the Velouté and lemon juice.
2. Soften the gelatin in a little water and heat until it is completely dissolved. Cool and add to the fish mixture. Season with salt and pepper to taste.
3. Beat the egg whites until stiff and fold into the fish mixture. Pour into a buttered mold and refrigerate for several hours, or until set. Slice to serve. Serve with tomato wedges, lemon wedges, and Rémoulade Sauce (see recipe p. 201).

Cold Fish Salad

6 SERVINGS

1 carrot, trimmed, scraped, and
    grated
1 onion, peeled and minced
1 celery stalk, trimmed and
    minced
1 green pepper, seeded and
    minced

1 pimiento, minced
½ to ¾ cup Mayonnaise (see
    recipe p. 200)
2 to 3 cups leftover poached fish
Salt
Freshly ground black pepper
Lemon juice

Combine all the vegetables with the Mayonnaise. Fold the fish into the mixture carefully. Season with salt, pepper, and lemon juice to taste. Chill and serve on lettuce leaves, garnished with parsley and tomatoes.

Escoffier Salad

6 SERVINGS

3 cups cooked roast beef, cut
    into julienne
1 onion, peeled and sliced thin
½ green pepper, sliced thin
1 small tomato, sliced thin
2 small dill pickles, sliced thin
2 tablespoons ketchup

1 teaspoon Dijon mustard
    Dash of Tabasco sauce
    Dash of Worcestershire sauce
    Salt to taste
    Freshly ground black pepper
    to taste

Combine all the ingredients in a bowl. Cover and refrigerate for a few hours to let the flavors develop. If the salad is not tart enough for you, add a little pickle juice.

NOTE: Any cooked meat can be used in this salad.

Chicken Salad

6 SERVINGS

2 to 3 cups diced cooked
    chicken
2 canned pineapple rings, diced
1 peach, peeled and diced
4 lettuce leaves, shredded
    Juice of ½ lemon
4 tablespoons heavy cream,
    whipped

4 tablespoons Mayonnaise (see
    recipe p. 200)
    Salt to taste
    Freshly ground black pepper
    to taste

Mix all the ingredients in a bowl. Serve on lettuce leaves and garnish with a pineapple slice and a tomato wedge, if desired.

Chicken Salad with White Asparagus

6 SERVINGS

2 cups diced cooked chicken
½ cup diced mushrooms
4 canned pineapple slices, diced
4 stalks canned white asparagus, diced
¼ cup Mayonnaise (see recipe p. 200)

¼ cup heavy cream, whipped
Salt to taste
Freshly ground black pepper to taste

Mix all the ingredients together in a bowl. Serve on shredded lettuce, garnished with asparagus spears, if desired.

Rice Salad

6 SERVINGS

3 cups cold cooked rice
½ cup diced canned pineapple
½ cup diced peeled apple
4 teaspoons curry powder
4 canned figs, diced

Salt to taste
Freshly ground black pepper to taste
Lettuce leaves
¼ cup toasted almond slices

Mix all the ingredients, except lettuce and almonds, together in a bowl. Let sit at room temperature for 1 to 2 hours to develop the flavor. Serve on lettuce leaves and sprinkle the toasted almond slices on top.

String Bean Casserole

6 SERVINGS

3 tablespoons butter or
    margarine
1 potato, peeled and thinly
    sliced
1 onion, peeled and sliced
1½ cups cooked string beans,
    chopped

Salt
Freshly ground black pepper
½ cup Chicken Stock (see
    recipe p. 58)
½ cup bread crumbs

1. Preheat the oven to 350 degrees.

2. Melt the butter in a frying pan. Add the potato and onion slices and sauté for 4 to 5 minutes. Add the beans and sauté for 1 minute. Season with salt and pepper to taste and add the stock and mix well.

3. Transfer the vegetables to a buttered baking dish. Sprinkle the bread crumbs on top and bake for 10 minutes, or until the top is golden brown.

Potato Crisps

6 SERVINGS

3 leftover baked potatoes
  Salt
  Freshly ground black pepper

1 cup butter or margarine,
    melted
1 cup dried bread crumbs

1. Preheat the oven to 450 degrees.

2. Peel the potatoes and slice them into 1-inch-thick rounds. Sprinkle the slices with salt and pepper.

3. Brush the potato slices on all sides with the melted butter. Dip them in the bread crumbs and put the slices on a buttered baking sheet. Bake for 15 minutes, or until brown and crisp. Serve hot.

Mashed Potato Patties

6 SERVINGS

2 cups leftover mashed potatoes
6 tablespoons chopped parsley
3 tablespoons all-purpose flour
2 small eggs

Salt
Freshly ground black pepper
6 tablespoons vegetable oil

Combine the potatoes, parsley, flour, and eggs. Season with salt and pepper to taste. Flour your hands slightly and form small patties out of the mixture. Fry them in hot oil until golden brown on both sides.

13

Desserts

Oranges in Strawberry Sauce, Pear Tart, and Amaretti Rice Mold
with Orange Sauce.

Most people eat desserts, even when they say they're on a
diet. There are not many people who can turn down a piece of
chocolate cake of a slice of cherry pie. Here is a whole group of
temptations for you to try.

Double Chocolate Cake

9 TO 12 SERVINGS

¾ cup butter or margarine
1 cup milk
2 ounces dark chocolate
1½ cups all-purpose flour
½ cup cocoa
1 tablespoon baking powder

3 eggs
1½ cups sugar
1 teaspoon vanilla extract
1 tablespoon brandy
Chocolate Icing (see recipe below)

1. Butter and flour two 9-inch springform pans. Set aside.
2. Heat the butter, milk, and dark chocolate together until they are melted and smooth. Cool to lukewarm.
3. Preheat the oven to 350 degrees.
4. Sift together the flour, cocoa, and baking powder.
5. Beat the eggs with the sugar until they are light and fluffy. Stir in the vanilla and brandy. Add the flour and the cooled chocolate mixture alternately to the eggs, beating after each addition.
6. Pour into the prepared pans and bake for 35 minutes, or until a cake tester comes out clean. Cool and remove from the pans. When cool, frost with Chocolate Icing.

Chocolate Icing

12 ounces dark (German Sweet) chocolate
2 teaspoons instant coffee powder

1½ cups heavy cream

1. Heat all the ingredients over low heat, stirring, until melted and smooth. Remove from the heat and let cool until thickened.
2. Put one layer of the cake on a cake rack. Spread with one third of the cooled icing. Cover with the second cake layer. Spread the rest of the icing on the sides and top of the cake. When the icing has set, remove the cake to a serving dish. Serve with sweetened whipped cream.

Sunken Cherry Cake

8 TO 10 SERVINGS

Streussel (see recipe below)
1 cup butter or margarine
1½ cups sugar
3 eggs
3 tablespoons kirsch

2½ cups all-purpose flour
½ cup cornstarch
2 teaspoons baking powder
1 large can pie cherries,
    drained

1. Butter and flour a 9-inch springform pan. Prepare the Streussel and set aside.

2. Preheat the oven to 375 degrees.

3. Cream the butter and sugar until light and fluffy. Add the eggs one at a time, beating after each addition. Stir in the kirsch.

4. Sift the flour, cornstarch, and baking powder together. Fold the mixture into the butter-egg mixture. Pour the batter into the prepared baking pan. Spread the drained cherries on top of the batter and press them down into the batter. Sprinkle the Streussel on top of the cake and bake for 1 hour, or until a cake tester comes out clean. Serve warm with sweetened whipped cream, if desired.

Streussel

¼ cup butter or margarine,
    softened
¼ cup sugar

¼ cup all-purpose flour
1 teaspoon ground cinnamon

Mix all the ingredients together with your fingers until the mixture forms small crumbs.

Orange Cake

8 TO 10 SERVINGS

Juice of 2 oranges
Juice of 1 lemon
Grand Marnier
1¼ cups all-purpose flour
3 teaspoons baking powder
1 cup butter or margarine
1⅓ cups sugar

3 eggs
¼ cup apricot jam
1 tablespoon water
Orange Buttercream (see
  recipe below)
1 can mandarin orange
  segments, drained

1. Preheat the oven to 350 degrees. Butter and flour two 9-inch springform pans.

2. Put the juices into a measuring cup and add Grand Marnier until the liquid measures ¾ cup.

3. Sift the flour and baking powder together.

4. Cream the butter and the sugar together until light and fluffy. Add the eggs one at a time, beating after each addition. Add the juices and flour alternately to the butter mixture until the ingredients are well combined. Pour the batter into the prepared pans and bake until a cake tester comes out clean.

5. Heat the apricot jam with the water and boil the mixture down a little. Cool.

6. When the cakes are done, invert on racks to cool.

7. Put one layer on a serving plate and sprinkle it with some Grand Marnier. Coat with a layer of Orange Buttercream. Put the second layer on top of the first and coat the top and sides of the cake with the apricot glaze. Frost completely with the remaining Orange Buttercream. Arrange the drained orange sections decoratively on top of the cake. Serve at room temperature.

Orange Buttercream

3 egg yolks
6 tablespoons plus ½ cup sugar
2 tablespoons cornstarch
¼ cup orange juice
¾ cup milk

1 pound butter or margarine,
  softened
2 to 3 tablespoons Grand
  Marnier

1. Mix the egg yolks, 6 tablespoons of sugar, cornstarch, and orange juice together in a bowl, beating to combine.

2. Heat the milk just to the boiling point. Whisk the yolk mixture into the milk and cook and stir until thick. Pour into a bowl, sprinkle the top with sugar (so a crust doesn't form) and cool.

3. Whip the butter and the remaining ½ cup sugar until light and soft. Mix in the cooled cream base. Add the Grand Marnier to taste and continue to whip until smooth.

Walnut Cream Cake

8 TO 10 SERVINGS

2 cups ground toasted walnuts
¼ cup cornstarch
1 teaspoon baking powder
6 egg yolks
½ cup sugar
1 tablespoon lemon juice

1 tablespoon Cognac
6 egg whites
Pinch of salt
Mocha Buttercream Frosting
(see recipe below)

1. Preheat the oven to 350 degrees. Butter and flour two 9-inch springform pans.

2. Mix the nuts, cornstarch, and baking powder together.

3. Beat the egg yolks with the sugar until thick and light. Fold in the lemon juice, nut mixture, and the Cognac.

4. Beat the egg whites with a pinch of salt until they are stiff. Fold the beaten egg whites into the batter. Pour the batter into the prepared pans and bake for about 40 minutes, or until a cake tester comes out clean. Cool the cakes completely and remove from the pans.

5. Put one layer on a serving plate and spread one third of the frosting on top. Add the second layer and spread the rest of the frosting on the top and sides of the cake.

Mocha Buttercream Frosting

1 cup plus 2 tablespoons sugar
1 tablespoon cornstarch
1 egg yolk
½ cup milk
½ pound butter or margarine, softened

1 tablespoon instant coffee powder dissolved in 1 teaspoon water and 1 teaspoon Kahlúa

1. Mix the 2 tablespoons of sugar, cornstarch, and egg yolk in a saucepan. Beat well to combine.
2. Heat the milk and add it to the custard base. Cook and stir over medium heat, until thickened. Pour into a bowl, sprinkle the top with a little sugar (so a crust doesn't form), and cool completely.
3. Cream the butter with 1 cup of sugar until it is very light. Add the cooled pastry cream a little at a time, beating constantly. Beat in the dissolved coffee powder.

German Apple Cake

6 TO 8 SERVINGS

1 recipe 1-2-3 Dough (see recipe p. 240)
4 to 5 large baking apples
½ cup unseasoned bread crumbs
½ cup heavy cream
Juice of 1 lemon

2 eggs
1 tablespoon cornstarch
½ cup sugar
¼ teaspoon vanilla extract
1 cup sour cream
½ cup apricot preserves, heated

1. Prepare the crust and refrigerate it while you are making the filling.
2. Peel the apples, core them, and cut them in half. Score the apples on the rounded sides and set aside.
3. Butter and flour a 9-inch springform pan. Press the chilled dough into the prepared pan to cover the bottom and come halfway up the sides of the pan. Sprinkle the bread crumbs evenly over the bottom crust.

4. Put the prepared apples in the pan, rounded side up. Fill the spaces with pieces of apple.

5. Mix the cream, lemon juice, eggs, cornstarch, sugar, vanilla, and sour cream together in a bowl. Beat with a whisk to combine well.

6. Preheat the oven to 375 degrees.

7. Pour the cream mixture over the apples and bake for 1 to 1½ hours, or until the apples are tender and the filling is set. Cool slightly and brush the top of the cake with the warm apricot preserves.

Cheesecake à la Maison

6 TO 8 SERVINGS

2 cups graham cracker crumbs
1½ cups plus 2 tablespoons sugar
8 tablespoons butter or
    margarine, melted
3 8-ounce packages cream
    cheese, softened

4 eggs
2 teaspoons vanilla extract
1 tablespoon lemon juice
1 pint strawberries, hulled

1. Preheat the oven to 350 degrees.

2. Combine the graham cracker crumbs and 2 tablespoons of sugar in a small bowl. Dribble the melted butter over the mixture and toss lightly. Press the crumbs firmly to the bottom and sides of an 8-inch springform pan. Refrigerate the pan while preparing the filling.

3. Beat the cream cheese, eggs, vanilla, and lemon juice together until smooth. Pour into the chilled crust. Bake for 45 minutes, turn the oven off, and let the cake cool in the oven.

4. To serve, remove the sides of the pan and put the cake on a serving plate. Arrange the strawberries attractively on top. The cake should be served chilled.

1-2-3 Dough

1 cup sugar
2 cups butter or margarine,
softened

3 cups all-purpose flour
1 egg

Combine the ingredients quickly to form a dough. Do not over-work the mixture. Cover and refrigerate for at least 1 hour before using.

NOTE: This recipe can be doubled easily, but it cannot be cut in half. The dough will keep for at least a week in the refrigerator if you cover it tightly.

Pear Tart

6 TO 8 SERVINGS

2 cups water
1¾ cups sugar
Juice of 1 lemon
Small piece of vanilla bean
2 pears, peeled, halved, and
cored
1 recipe 1-2-3 Dough (see
recipe p. 240)

2 tablespoons all-purpose flour
or cornstarch
1 cup light cream or milk
1 teaspoon vanilla extract
4 egg yolks
½ cup apricot jam, heated
¼ cup blanched almond slices
(optional)

1. Bring the water, 1 cup of sugar, lemon juice, and piece of vanilla bean to a boil. Simmer for 5 minutes and add the pear halves. Lower the heat to simmer and poach the pears until they are barely tender. Remove from the heat and let the pears cool in the liquid.

2. Prepare the dough and line a tart pan with it. Bake blind in a 400-degree oven for 15 minutes, or until golden brown. Remove from the oven and set aside to cool.

3. Combine the flour, cream, vanilla, ¾ cup of sugar, and the egg yolks in a saucepan. Bring to a boil, stirring constantly. Cool quickly by putting the saucepan into a pan of cracked ice.

4. Remove the pears from the poaching liquid and let them drain.

5. Pour the cooled pastry cream into the prepared shell. Slice the pears and arrange them over the pastry cream (see p. 233). Brush the apricot jam over the top of the tart and sprinkle the almond slices, if desired, over the tart. Chill until ready to serve.

Swiss Lemon Tart

6 TO 8 SERVINGS

¾ cup butter or margarine,
   softened
1¼ cups flour
1 egg yolk
4 eggs
¾ cup sugar
⅔ cup lemon juice

½ cup orange juice
   Grated peel of 2 lemons
¼ cup heavy cream
   Lemon segments
¼ cup apricot jam
1 tablespoon water

1. Put ½ cup butter into a mixing bowl and add the flour. Cut the butter into the flour, using a pastry blender or two knives, until the mixture resembles coarse meal. Add the egg yolk and combine until the mixture leaves the sides of the bowl and forms a ball. Work quickly and do not overwork the dough. Cover the bowl and refrigerate the dough for ½ hour.

2. Preheat the oven to 400 degrees.

3. Butter a 10-inch tart pan and roll the dough out to fit it. Line the dough with a sheet of aluminum foil. Spread a layer of dried beans over the foil and bake the tart shell for 10 minutes. Remove the beans and the foil and bake the shell for 15 minutes longer, or until the crust is lightly colored. Remove from the oven and cool. Lower the oven temperature to 375 degrees.

4. Mix the eggs, sugar, lemon and orange juices, and lemon peel together in a bowl. Beat to combine well.

5. Heat ¼ cup of butter and the cream together in a saucepan and add the egg mixture. Cook, stirring, until thick. Cool slightly and pour the filling into the prepared crust. Bake for 20 minutes. Remove from the oven and cool. Garnish with lemon segments.

6. Heat the apricot jam and water together in a small saucepan. Boil the mixture down a little. Cool slightly and brush over the top of the tart.

Blueberry Tart

6 TO 8 SERVINGS

1 recipe 1-2-3 Dough (see recipe p. 240)
2 tablespoons all-purpose flour or cornstarch
1 cup light cream or milk
1 teaspoon vanilla extract
¾ cup sugar
4 egg yolks
1 cup fresh blueberries
¼ cup apricot jam
1 tablespoon water

1. Prepare the dough and line a tart pan with it. Bake blind in a 400-degree oven for 15 minutes, or until golden brown.
2. Combine the flour, cream, vanilla, sugar, and egg yolks in a saucepan. Bring to a boil, stirring constantly. Cool quickly by putting the saucepan into a pan of cracked ice.
3. Pour the cooled pastry cream into the prepared shell and put the blueberries on top.
4. Heat the apricot jam with the water and boil the mixture down a little. Cool slightly and brush the glaze over the blueberries. Chill the tart for 1 to 2 hours before serving.

Swiss Cherry Pie

6 TO 8 SERVINGS

1 recipe 1-2-3 Dough (see recipe p. 240)
Unseasoned bread crumbs
1 pound fresh pitted cherries, or 1 large can pitted pie cherries, drained
½ cup sour cream
½ cup heavy cream
1 teaspoon cornstarch
¼ cup sugar (more or less, depending on the sweetness of the cherries)
Juice of ½ lemon
1 egg

1. Prepare the dough and line the pie pan with it. Sprinkle a thin layer of bread crumbs over the bottom crust. Put the cherries on the bottom of the crust.

2. Preheat the oven to 375 degrees.

3. Mix the sour cream, heavy cream, cornstarch, sugar, lemon juice, and egg together in a bowl until well blended. Pour over the cherries and bake for 1 hour.

Cherry Cheese Tart

8 TO 10 SERVINGS

1 recipe 1-2-3 Dough (see recipe p. 240)
½ cup unseasoned bread crumbs
4 egg yolks
⅔ cup sugar
2 8-ounce packages farmer cheese

1½ cups sour cream
5 teaspoons cornstarch
1 teaspoon vanilla extract
Grated peel of 2 lemons
Juice of ½ lemon
4 egg whites
1 large can sour pie cherries, drained

1. Prepare the dough and use it to line a buttered 9-inch spring-form pan, pressing the dough three quarters of the way up the sides of the pan. Sprinkle the bottom of the dough with the bread crumbs.

2. Preheat the oven to 400 degrees.

3. Beat the egg yolks and sugar together until light and fluffy.

4. Whip the farmer cheese until it is light and smooth and add it to the egg yolk mixture with the sour cream. Beat in the cornstarch, vanilla, grated peel, and lemon juice.

5. Beat the egg whites until stiff and fold them into the cheese mixture.

6. Spread the drained cherries over the bottom of the prepared crust. Pour the cheese mixture over the cherries and bake for 50 to 60 minutes, or until set. If the top puffs up very high during the baking, remove the tart from the oven after about 40 minutes and slit the top in the center to allow some of the steam to escape. Return to the oven to finish the baking. If the top begins to brown too quickly, cover the tart with a piece of aluminum foil. Cool the tart in the pan before removing the sides. Serve with sweetened whipped cream, if desired.

1-2-3 Cookies

Make the 1-2-3 Dough (see recipe p. 240) and divide it in half. Add 2 tablespoons of cocoa to one half of the dough. Roll out each half into a square and place one square on top of the other. Roll up as you would a jelly roll and chill for ½ hour. Cut into ½-inch-thick slices and put the slices on a buttered and floured cookie sheet. Bake in a 375-degree oven for 15 to 20 minutes.

Chocolate Soufflé

6 SERVINGS

2 tablespoons butter
2 tablespoons all-purpose flour
½ cup milk
3 tablespoons sugar
1½ ounces semisweet chocolate

2 egg yolks
3 egg whites
  Chocolate Sauce (see recipe below)

1. Melt the butter in a small heavy saucepan. Add the flour all at once, stirring until the mixture is smooth and creamy. Remove from the heat and let the *roux* cool.

2. Heat the milk, sugar, and chocolate until the chocolate melts. Pour the chocolate mixture into the cooled *roux*, stirring constantly. Return to the heat and stir over moderate heat until well blended and thick. Remove from the heat and let cool.

3. Beat in the egg yolks one at a time.

4. Beat the egg whites until stiff and fold them into the cooled chocolate mixture.

5. Preheat the oven to 325 degrees.

6. Butter a 1-quart soufflé dish very well. Sprinkle sugar over the inside of the dish so that it is thoroughly coated with both butter and sugar. Pour in the soufflé mixture and bake for 40 minutes, or until the top springs back when you touch it. Serve with Chocolate Sauce.

Chocolate Sauce

1 cup bittersweet chocolate bits   ½ cup heavy cream

Combine the chocolate and cream in the top of a double boiler over simmering water. Stir until the chocolate melts and the sauce is smooth.

Hot Lemon Soufflé

6 SERVINGS

¼ cup butter or margarine   4 egg yolks
½ cup sugar   5 egg whites
6 tablespoons lemon juice   Confectioner's sugar
  Grated peel of 2 lemons

1. Combine the butter, ¼ cup sugar, the lemon juice, and lemon peel in a heavy pan, stirring over medium heat until the butter is melted and the sugar dissolved. Remove from the heat and beat in the egg yolks one at a time. Return to the heat and cook over low heat, stirring constantly, until the mixture thickens to the consistency of whipping cream.
2. Preheat the oven to 425 degrees. Butter a 1½-quart soufflé dish very well. Sprinkle the inside of the dish with sugar, making sure to coat the entire surface.
3. Whip the egg whites until stiff. Fold the remaining ¼ cup of sugar into the beaten egg whites. Fold one quarter of the egg whites into the soufflé base, then add the mixture to the remaining egg whites and fold in gently.
4. Spoon the soufflé into the prepared dish, smooth the top, and bake for 12 to 15 minutes, or until the soufflé is puffed and browned. Sprinkle with confectioner's sugar and serve at once with sweetened whipped cream.

Mocha-Walnut Souffle

6 SERVINGS

2 tablespoons instant coffee
   powder
2 tablespoons cocoa
½ cup sugar
1 cup milk
3 tablespoons butter or
   margarine

4 tablespoons all-purpose flour
6 egg yolks
2 tablespoons Cognac
½ cup chopped walnuts
7 egg whites

1. Butter and sugar a 1½-quart soufflé dish. You can add a collar, if you want, but make sure you butter and sugar it also.

2. Heat the coffee powder, cocoa, sugar, and milk together until the dry ingredients are dissolved.

3. Melt the butter and add the flour all at once, stirring until the mixture is smooth and creamy. Stir in the milk mixture and cook, stirring, until the custard thickens. Remove from the heat. Beat in the egg yolks one at a time, beating well after each addition. Stir in the Cognac and walnuts.

4. Preheat the oven to 375 degrees.

5. Whip the egg whites with a pinch of sugar until they are stiff. Fold the egg whites into the soufflé base and pour the soufflé into the prepared dish. Bake for 25 minutes. The soufflé will still be a little moist in the center. If you like a dry soufflé, bake for 5 or 10 minutes longer.

Nancy's Custard

8 SERVINGS

4 cups milk
   Pieces of vanilla bean
½ cup sugar

Pinch of salt
6 egg yolks

1. Scald the milk with the vanilla bean. Stir in the sugar and the salt.

2. Beat the egg yolks until very well combined. Stir a little hot milk into the beaten egg yolks, then pour the yolks into the hot milk, stirring constantly.

3. Preheat the oven to 325 degrees.

4. Strain the custard mixture into eight individual cups. Put the custard cups in a roasting pan and pour enough hot water into the pan to come halfway up the sides of the cups. Bake for 1½ hours, or until the custard is firm. Remove the cups from the roasting pan, cool, and chill for several hours. Serve cold.

Bavarian Cream

6 SERVINGS

4 egg yolks
2 cups milk
½ cup sugar
2 tablespoons unflavored
    gelatin

Grand Marnier, kirsch, puréed
    strawberries, or puréed
    raspberries for flavoring
    (optional)
1 cup heavy cream, whipped

1. Put the egg yolks and ½ cup of milk in a saucepan and beat to combine well. Set aside.

2. Bring the rest of the milk and the sugar just to the boiling point in another saucepan. Add the hot milk to the egg yolk mixture, beating constantly over medium heat. Add the gelatin and continue to beat. Remove from the heat and strain the custard into a clean bowl. Put in a cool place and stir once or twice so a crust does not form.

3. Before the custard thickens completely, add the flavoring, if desired, and fold in the whipped cream. Pour the custard into serving glasses and chill.

Amaretti Rice Mold

6 SERVINGS

1 tablespoon butter or
     margarine
¾ cup raw rice
3 cups milk
     Pinch of salt
10 amaretti cookies
     Peel of 1 orange

½ cup sugar
¼ cup flour
4 egg yolks, beaten
4 egg whites
     Orange Sauce (see recipe
        below)

1. Melt the butter in a saucepan and add the rice. Stir to coat the rice with the butter. Add the milk and salt and bring to a boil. Lower the heat and simmer, stirring occasionally, until all the milk is absorbed. This will take about 40 minutes. Cool the rice mixture.

2. Preheat the oven to 400 degrees.

3. Put the cookies, orange peel, sugar, and flour into the container of a food processor and grind.

4. Mix the egg yolks into the cooled rice mixture and stir in the cookie mixture.

5. Beat the egg whites with a pinch of sugar until stiff. Fold into the rice mixture. Pour into a buttered and sugared 2-quart soufflé dish. Bake for 35 to 40 minutes. Unmold the pudding or serve it from the dish. The pudding can be served hot or warm with warm Orange Sauce.

Orange Sauce

1 tablespoon cornstarch
¼ cup lemon juice
½ cup sugar
     Grated peel of 1 orange

1 tablespoon butter
1 cup orange juice
1 egg yolk, beaten
3 tablespoons Grand Marnier

1. Mix the cornstarch with the lemon juice and stir to dissolve the cornstarch.

2. Put the sugar, orange peel, butter, and orange juice into a saucepan. Bring to a boil and add the cornstarch mixture. Simmer for 3 to 4 minutes.

3. Add a little of the hot liquid to the egg yolk, then beat the egg yolk into the sauce. Cook, stirring, for 2 minutes. Remove from the heat and stir in the Grand Marnier. Serve warm.

German Bread Pudding

6 SERVINGS

2 cups milk
2 eggs
3 tablespoons sugar
6 stale seedless rolls, sliced
1 pound baking apples, peeled, cored, and sliced

½ cup raisins
4 tablespoons butter, cut into small pieces
Vanilla Sauce (see recipe below)

1. Preheat the oven to 375 degrees. Butter a 1½-quart soufflé dish very well.

2. Put the milk, eggs, and sugar in a saucepan. Beat to combine well and cook over medium heat until slightly thickened. Set aside.

3. Make layers in the soufflé dish of first the rolls, then the apple slices, sprinkling each layer with some raisins. End the layers with apples. Dot the apples with the butter pieces and pour on the custard. Bake for 1 hour, or until firm. Serve with Vanilla Sauce.

Vanilla Sauce

2 cups milk
½ vanilla bean
½ cup sugar

2 teaspoons cornstarch dissolved in 4 teaspoons water
2 egg yolks, beaten

Bring the milk, vanilla bean, and sugar to a boil. Add the dissolved cornstarch and bring to a boil again. Cook for 3 to 4 minutes and add the egg yolks, stirring to combine well. Serve.

Farina Pudding

6 SERVINGS

3 cups milk
2 tablespoons sugar
Dash of vanilla extract
1 cup Cream of Wheat

1 cup raisins
2 egg whites
Apple slices for garnish

1. Put the milk in a saucepan and bring to a boil. Gradually add the sugar and the vanilla. Stir well. Add the cream of wheat and cook over medium heat for 15 minutes. Add the raisins and cook for 15 minutes longer. Remove from the heat and cool completely.
2. Beat the egg whites until stiff and fold them gently into the Cream of Wheat.
3. Sprinkle individual custard cups with sugar and fill with the pudding. Refrigerate for at least 8 hours before serving. When ready to serve, unmold on individual serving plates and garnish with fresh apple slices.

Frozen Zabaglione

6 SERVINGS

5 egg yolks
5 tablespoons sugar
½ cup dry Marsala

¼ cup white rum
2 cups heavy cream
¼ cup confectioner's sugar

1. Put the egg yolks and granulated sugar in the top of a double boiler. Beat to combine well. Stir in the Marsala and rum and put the pot over boiling water. Beat until very thick. Remove from the heat and wrap the pot in a cold towel. Stir constantly until the mixture cools.
2. Beat the cream and confectioner's sugar until stiff. Fold into the cooled egg yolk base. Pour the custard into individual molds or a ring mold. Freeze until firm. Unmold and serve with fresh fruit, if desired.

Frozen Banana Soufflé

8 TO 10 SERVINGS

5 egg yolks
½ cup plus 2 tablespoons sugar
1 cup heavy cream
2⅓ cups mashed bananas

1 to 2 tablespoons light rum
1 teaspoon lemon juice
Pinch of nutmeg
5 egg whites

1. Put the egg yolks and ½ cup sugar in the top of a double boiler. Put over boiling water and beat with a whisk until thick and light in color. Remove from the heat and continue to beat until the mixture cools a little.

2. Whip the cream until stiff and set it aside.

3. Purée the bananas with the rum and lemon juice. Add to the cooled egg yolk mixture with the nutmeg.

4. Beat the egg whites until foamy. Add the remaining 2 tablespoons of sugar and beat until stiff.

5. Fold the egg whites and the whipped cream into the banana base. Pour into a collared soufflé dish or a 9-inch springform pan. Freeze for at least 6 hours. Serve with sweetened whipped cream, Chocolate Sauce (see recipe p. 245), and/or toasted sliced almonds.

Cold Apricot Soufflé

6 TO 8 SERVINGS

1 bag (12 ounces) dried
      apricots
¼ cup water
2 tablespoons brandy
   Dash of vanilla
1½ teaspoons unflavored gelatin
   Juice of 1 lemon

4 eggs
3 egg yolks
⅔ cup sugar
2½ cups heavy cream
   Sweetened whipped cream
      for garnish

1. Combine the apricots and water and cook until the apricots are tender. Cool and drain well. Purée in a blender or food processor with the brandy and vanilla. Set aside.

2. Soften the gelatin in the lemon juice and then heat until the gelatin is completely dissolved. Cool.

3. Beat the eggs, egg yolks, and sugar until very light and doubled in volume. Blend in the apricot purée and the gelatin.

4. Whip the cream lightly and fold it into the apricot mixture. Pour into a 9-inch springform pan. Refrigerate for a few hours, or until firm. Remove the sides of the pan and decorate the soufflé with sweetened whipped cream. Refrigerate until serving time.

NOTE: The soufflé may also be poured into individual serving dishes and decorated with whipped cream at serving time.

Mocha Mousse

6 SERVINGS

2 cups milk
2 tablespoons sugar
2 tablespoons instant coffee
      powder
2 tablespoons cornstarch
      dissolved in 4 tablespoons
      water

2 cups heavy cream
   Chocolate shavings or instant
      coffee powder for garnish

1. Heat the milk until it is warm. Add the sugar and coffee powder. Bring to a boil and stir in the cornstarch mixture. Cook and stir until thickened. Remove from the heat, chill, and pour into a cool clean bowl. Sprinkle the top with sugar to prevent a crust from forming. Cool the mixture completely.

2. Whip the cream into stiff peaks. Gently fold it into the cooled custard. Pour the mousse into serving glasses and chill. Serve topped with chocolate shavings or instant coffee powder.

Lemon Mousse

6 SERVINGS

½ cup lemon juice
2 teaspoons grated lemon peel
½ cup sugar

4 egg yolks, beaten
1 cup heavy cream, whipped

Heat the lemon juice, lemon peel, sugar, and egg yolks together in a saucepan. Cook and stir until thickened. Cool and fold in the whipped cream. Chill before serving.

Chocolate Mousse

6 SERVINGS

5 ounces sweet chocolate
½ cup heavy cream, whipped
4 egg whites, beaten stiff

Brandy
Kahlúa

Melt the chocolate in the top of a double boiler over simmering water. When it is melted, cool it to lukewarm. Fold the whipped cream and beaten egg whites into the cooled chocolate and flavor with brandy and Kahlúa to taste. Chill before serving.

Orange Cream Mold

6 SERVINGS

1 tablespoon unflavored gelatin
¼ cup fresh orange juice
3 eggs
¾ cup sugar

1 teaspoon grated orange peel
½ grated lemon peel
1 tablespoon lemon juice
1 cup heavy cream

1. Mix the gelatin with the orange juice in a small saucepan. Let stand a few minutes to soften the gelatin. Then heat until the gelatin is dissolved completely. Cool.

2. Beat the eggs with the sugar and citrus peels. When doubled in volume, beat in the gelatin and lemon juice.

3. Whip the heavy cream until it is stiff and blend it into the egg mixture. Pour into a mold and chill for at least 3 hours, or until set. Unmold and serve with orange segments and fresh strawberries.

Black Forest Apples

8 SERVINGS

8 apples
8 tablespoons raisins
8 tablespoons sliced almonds

8 tablespoons honey
8 tablespoons kirsch

1. Preheat the oven to 350 degrees.

2. Cut a lid off each of the apples and reserve it. Peel each apple one third of the way down. Core the apple with a melon ball cutter, being careful not to cut through the bottom of the apple.

3. Fill each apple with 1 tablespoon of raisins and almonds. Pour 1 tablespoon of honey into each apple and sprinkle 1 tablespoon of kirsch over each apple. Put the tops back on the apples.

4. Put the apples into a baking pan and pour in about ¼ inch of water. Bake for 25 minutes, or until the apples are tender.

Banana Flambé

6 SERVINGS

3 bananas
3 tablespoons butter
¾ cup sugar
Juice of 1 orange

Juice of 1 lemon
4 tablespoons Grand Marnier
½ cup toasted almond slices

Peel the bananas and cut them in half lengthwise. Melt the butter in a frying pan and sauté the banana halves until they are lightly colored. Remove the bananas and add the sugar, orange juice, lemon juice, and Grand Marnier to the butter. Bring to a boil, and boil until the sugar dissolves. Return the bananas to the pan and simmer for a few minutes. Serve over vanilla ice cream. Sprinkle each serving with toasted almond slices.

Oranges in Strawberry Sauce

6 SERVINGS

1 pint strawberries, hulled and
    sliced
½ cup sugar
3 tablespoons Grand Marnier

6 oranges
½ cup toasted almond slices
⅓ cup currants or raisins,
    chopped

1. Macerate the strawberries in the sugar and Grand Marnier for several hours. Purée in a blender.
2. Peel the oranges completely. Slice them thin and seed them. Pour some of the strawberry purée on each individual plate and put the orange slices on top in a circle. Sprinkle the orange slices with the almonds and currants and refrigerate.

Brandied Peaches

8 TO 10 SERVINGS

4 cups water
1 cup sugar
1 cinnamon stick
  Peel of ½ orange

Peel of ½ lemon
8 to 10 whole peaches, washed
6 tablespoons brandy
6 tablespoons Grand Marnier

1. Bring the water, sugar, and cinnamon stick to a boil and add the orange and lemon peels. Add the peaches and poach for 6 to 8 minutes, depending on the ripeness of the peaches. Remove the peaches, let them cool, and peel them. Put them in a glass bowl.

2. Bring the poaching liquid back to a boil and add the brandy and Grand Marnier. Strain and pour over the peaches. Make sure the peaches are completely covered by liquid. Refrigerate, covered, for a few days to develop the flavor. Serve the peaches with ice cream.

Peach Melba

6 SERVINGS

1 package frozen raspberries in
  syrup, thawed
¼ cup sugar
1 tablespoon cornstarch,
  dissolved in 2 tablespoons
  water

Framboise
6 canned peach halves, drained
Vanilla ice cream
Sweetened whipped cream

1. Drain the thawed raspberries, reserving the syrup. Heat the raspberry syrup and sugar in a small saucepan until the liquid comes to a boil. Add the cornstarch mixture and stir and cook for a few minutes until the syrup thickens and clears. Add the drained raspberries and a drop or two of framboise.

2. Put a peach half in the bottom of a serving dish. Add a scoop of vanilla ice cream and pour some raspberry sauce over the ice cream. Decorate with sweetened whipped cream. Serve immediately.

Poires Belle Hélène

6 SERVINGS

2 cups water
1 cup sugar
  Juice of 1 lemon
  Small piece of cinnamon stick
3 pears, peeled, halved, and
  cored

Vanilla ice cream
Chocolate Sauce (see recipe
  p. 245)
Toasted almond slices
Sweetened whipped cream

1. Bring the water, sugar, lemon juice, and cinnamon stick to a boil. Simmer for 5 minutes and add the pear halves. Lower the heat to simmer and poach the pears until they are barely tender. Remove from the heat and let the pears cool in the liquid.

2. To serve, remove the pears from the poaching liquid and place one pear half in a dish. Top with 1 or 2 scoops of ice cream. Pour some hot Chocolate Sauce over the ice cream and sprinkle on some almonds. Top with sweetened whipped cream. Serve at once.

Strawberry Cream

6 SERVINGS

2 pints strawberries, hulled
1 cup sour cream
3 to 4 tablespoons sugar
  Juice of ½ lemon

1 cup heavy cream
  Whipped cream and
  strawberries for garnish

1. Purée enough strawberries to make 1 cup of purée. Mix the purée with the sour cream, sugar, and lemon juice.

2. Whip the cream until stiff. Fold the whipped cream into the strawberry mixture. Serve with whipped cream on top and a whole strawberry as garnish.

Raspberries Grand Duc

6 SERVINGS

1½ cups milk
   Piece of vanilla bean
 4 egg yolks
 ½ cup sugar
 ¼ cup all-purpose flour

5 egg whites
   Framboise
1 pint fresh raspberries
   Sweetened whipped cream
   (optional)

1. Heat 1 cup of milk with the vanilla bean.

2. Mix together the egg yolks, sugar, flour, and the remaining milk. Beat to combine well. Add the yolk mixture to the hot milk and cook, stirring until thick. Let the custard boil for a few minutes, then remove from the heat and let it cool completely. (If you sprinkle a little sugar on top of the custard, a skin will not form.) When the custard is cool, strain it into a clean bowl.

3. Beat the egg whites until stiff and fold them into the custard. Flavor with a few spoonfuls of framboise and chill.

4. To serve, put the custard in individual glass dishes. Put some raspberries on top and sprinkle them with a little framboise. Serve with sweetened whipped cream, if desired.

14

Tips from Tell

There are lots of things I've learned over the years, little secrets that make my work easier. I think they will help to make your time in the kitchen nicer, so I'm going to pass some of these tips on to you.

The tips are arranged in alphabetical order by key words, such as CREAM—Whipping, HERBS—Storing, and MEAT—Cutting. So, suppose you want to know what I've got to say about chicken stock. Do you look under CHICKEN? No! You look under STOCK—that's the key word.

I hope these tips help you as they helped me.

BREADING—I use the two-handed method, one wet and one dry. This is how it's done: You put some flour on a piece of wax paper. You beat eggs in a flat soup plate. And you put some bread crumbs on a piece of wax paper. You take the thing you want to bread in one hand and you dip it in the flour. Using the same hand, you dip it into the eggs, then drop it in the bread crumbs. With your other hand you coat it with bread crumbs. So, you have one wet hand and one dry hand and you will not bread your fingers. Try it and see!

CHICKEN STOCK—See STOCK.

CLAMS—Cleaning. Clams are very sandy, so you have to be sure to remove as much sand as possible or you will have a gritty dish. Dump the clams into a large pot. Fill the pot with lukewarm water, not too cold and not too hot—just nice. Let the clams sit in the water for 15 minutes or so. Then lift them out and pour out the water. You will see how sandy it is. Clean out the pot and put the clams back in. Fill the pot with lukewarm water again and let the clams sit for 15 minutes. When you take the clams out this time, hold them under lukewarm running water and scrub the shells all over with a stiff brush—a nail brush or a vegetable brush will do. Clean the pot out again and fill it with water. But this time, add ½ cup vinegar to the water before you add the clams. Let them sit in the vinegar water for 15 minutes before you take them out. The clams should be clean now, and you can cook them immediately or put them back in lukewarm water until you are ready to cook them.

CREAM—Whipping. When I'm asked how one can tell when cream is whipped enough, I usually answer that that point is reached 2 minutes before it's overwhipped! Really, you can tell when cream is whipped enough by stopping beating and seeing if the cream stays on the beaters. If it does, it's whipped enough.

CURRY POWDER—Curry powder is sometimes a little tricky to handle because some of the spices in the mixture contain natural sugar. When you sauté the curry powder this sugar starts to caramelize and turn bitter. To prevent this, you have to add some liquid to the pan right after you add the curry powder.

DEGLAZE—When meat is sautéed, it gives up some of its juices to the pan. These juices cook right along with the meat and they get very brown, and very concentrated. Sometimes they even form a shiny coating—and that's how we get to "deglaze." We want to lift this glaze, so we add a little wine, stock, or even water to the pan and stir with a wooden spoon, scraping up this glaze to add both color and flavor to the sauce.

EGG WHITES—Beating stiff. One way to tell if the egg whites are stiff enough is to turn the bowl upside down. If the egg whites don't fall out, they are fine. If you don't like that way, you can cut through the beaten egg whites with a knife. If the cut stays open, the whites are stiff enough.

HOLLANDAISE SAUCE—See SAUCE.

HERBS—Storing. Put the herbs on a cookie sheet and dry them in a 400-degree oven for a few minutes. Cool, crush, and pour into a jar. If you seal the jar tight and keep it out of direct sun and away from the heat, the herbs will keep better.

JUICE—Lemons and Oranges. Before you cut the lemon or orange in half to squeeze it, roll it on a flat surface, pressing down on it with the palm of your hand. This will soften the inside of the lemon so that it will be easier to squeeze and you will get more juice out of it.

MEAT—Tenderizing. I like to tenderize the meat I'm going to sauté by pounding it before I cook it. No, I don't beat at it as if I were pounding in a nail. I just pound it a little with a meat mallet to break down the cell structure. Remember—just a little.

MEAT—Roasting and Resting. Never put a roast of beef, pork, or veal directly into a hot oven. You must first seal in the juices. Heat a little oil in your roasting pan and brown the roast on all sides in the hot oil. Then put it into the oven to cook. This way the juices will stay inside the roast and it will taste much better. But don't do this with a standing rib roast, because rib roast has a fat layer on one side and a bone layer on the other, and these seal and protect the meat. Put a rib roast into a hot oven for 30 minutes, then turn down the temperature to finish cooking the rib roast. The high temperature does what the browning in oil does for other cuts. *Resting:* You should always let a roast stand for 10 to 15 minutes before you carve it. This allows the juices to settle back into the meat. If you carve a roast that has just come from the oven, the juices will run out onto the carving board; your meat will be dry, and only your carving board will be juicy. *Note:* You should also rest turkey, chicken, and other fowl before you carve them—for the same reason.

MUSSELS—Cleaning. Mussels are cleaned basically in the same way clams are, but with one more step. The mussels have to be scraped with a knife to remove their beards and any little barnacles that are stuck to them.

SALAD DRESSING—Always put the vinegar, salt, pepper, and herbs on salad greens before you add the oil. If you put the oil on first, it coats the leaves and the other flavors won't get through.

SAUCES—Cream Sauce. Lots of people don't like to make cream sauces because they always turn out lumpy. Well, here is a trick that will give you lump-free sauce every time. After you make your roux—that is, the butter-flour mixture—you let the *roux* cool a little. Then you heat whatever liquid your recipe calls for just until it comes to a boil and you add the hot liquid slowly to the *roux*, stirring constantly. Then you put the sauce back on the heat and cook until it is as thick as you want it. You should cook the sauce, for about 15 minutes to get rid of the flour taste.

SAUCES—Hollandaise. If your Hollandaise Sauce breaks down and separates, it is because your ingredients were either too hot or too cold. You can tell which by testing the sauce with your finger. If the sauce feels too hot, put an egg yolk or a little cold liquid into a clean bowl and beat in the Hollandaise slowly. If the sauce feels too cold, add a little hot water to a clean bowl and beat in the sauce slowly. Sometimes adding a little acid, such as vinegar or lemon juice, or even a little dry white wine, will help to restore the Hollandaise.

SAUCES—To Thicken. If your sauce turns out too thin and you don't have time to reduce it, you can thicken it with cornstarch. The cornstarch mixture should be 1:2—in other words, 1 tablespoon of cornstarch dissolved in 2 tablespoons of water. Bring your sauce to a boil and stir in some of the cornstarch mixture. The sauce should thicken in a minute or two. If it is still too thin, add more of the cornstarch mixture. The reason I don't tell you to use flour to thicken the sauce is that you would have to cook the sauce for 10 to 15 minutes to get rid of the flour taste. Cornstarch thickens the sauce almost immediately and doesn't affect its taste very much.

SAUCES—To Save. Sometimes you do all the right things and still the sauce doesn't turn out right. What can you do? If the sauce is lumpy, you can pour it through a strainer, pushing it through with a spoon or ladle, or you can put it in a blender and purée it for a few seconds. Then return the sauce to the pan and heat for a bit. If the sauce is too thick, you can thin it with a little stock, cream, or milk, adding the thinning agent a spoonful at a time until you get the desired consistency.

SEASONING FOOD—You should season your food at three different stages in the cooking process. Add one third of the seasoning when you begin to cook the dish. Then, about halfway through, add another third. Add the rest of the seasoning just before you serve. If you don't add some seasoning at the beginning, the food will not develop the proper flavor. The reason that you shouldn't add all the seasoning at the beginning is that if you boil down a sauce or a liquid too much, you may find you've used too much seasoning. You can always add more seasoning, but it's very hard to remove it once it's there. If, for some reason, you do add too much seasoning to a dish, you can drain off half the liquid and add water to compensate. Your sauce will be thinner, but it will taste much better. (Don't throw away the sauce you have poured off. It can be used at another time.) Another thing you can do is to add a raw potato to an overseasoned soup or stew, since potatoes tend to absorb seasonings and they may do the trick for you. But don't try to add a potato to tomato sauce. It won't affect it a bit. If you overseason a tomato sauce, you will have to prepare a small batch of unseasoned sauce and cook it down a little and then add it to the larger amount of sauce.

SEASONING—A Pan. The reason you season a new pan is so food won't stick to it when you cook. Seasoning is easy. You put a layer of salt in the pan—let's say 1 cup for a medium-size frying pan—and keep the pan over high heat until it gets very hot. The salt will begin to brown. This should take from 20 to 30 minutes. Put several layers of newspaper on a work surface and put the hot pan on the newspapers and let it cool for a few minutes. Take some newspaper and crumple it into a ball. Use the ball of newspaper to rub the inside of the pan in a circular motion. Use elbow grease and rub that salt into the pan, but don't burn yourself. Throw the salt and the ball of newspaper away and add ½ cup of vegetable oil to the pan. Return the pan to high heat and heat until the oil reaches the smoking point. Tilt the pan so that the oil gets all over the inside of the pan. Remove the pan from the heat and let it cool a little. Carefully pour out the oil and wipe the pan out with a towel—and you have a seasoned pan. There are two things you should remember when using a seasoned pan. First always heat the pan before you add anything to it. Second, never wash a seasoned pan. Just wipe it out with a dry towel and put it away. Remember, never wash a seasoned pan.

SPICES—Buying and Storing. Buy your spices in the smallest amounts possible. Dried spices don't keep their flavors longer than about eight months. Try to store your spices out of direct sunlight in a cool, dry spot. They will keep longer that way. You don't have to keep lots of exotic spices on hand for everyday cooking, but there are some you should have, such as allspice, basil, bay leaves, caraway seeds, chili powder, cinnamon (ground and stick), cloves (ground and whole), curry powder, fennel seeds, ginger, juniper berries, marjoram, mustard powder, nutmeg, oregano, paprika, pepper (white and black), poultry seasoning, rosemary, saffron, tarragon, and thyme.

SPICES—Substituting dried for fresh. The general rule here is to use half as much of a dried spice or herb when you are substituting for the fresh.

STOCK—Degreasing. The best, and easiest, way to degrease a stock is to chill it so the fat rises to the top. Then you can just lift it off. If you don't have time to do that, you can take a small spoon and, making small circles on the top of the stock, scoop the fat off a little at a time. It will take a while, but you should be able to get most of the fat off. If there is any left, crumple up a paper towel and brush it across the top of the stock to pick up the rest of the fat.

STOCK—To Keep. There are two ways you can keep stock. You can freeze it in 1- or 2-cup covered containers, or you can store it in jars in the refrigerator. If you are refrigerating it only, don't remove the fat layer, because the fat will act as a preservative and you will be able to keep the stock in the refrigerator for about a week without its breaking down. Once you remove that layer of fat, the stock will begin to break down. You then have to reboil it, use it immediately, or throw it out.

WINE—Cooking With. When a recipe calls for wine, don't use supermarket cooking wines because they contain salt and will unbalance the taste of your dish. Use a table wine instead. The best thing to do is to buy a few bottles of table wine and keep them on hand for cooking. They don't have to be expensive (house brands at your liquor store will do) and they will keep well if they are refrigerated.

Glossary

Arrowroot A finely ground starch used for thickening.

Aspic A clear jelly made from meat, poultry, or fish stock mixed with gelatin.

Au Gratin Food that has been covered with a sauce and then sprinkled with grated cheese or bread crumbs before baking.

Au Jus Food served with a sauce made from natural juices.

Bain Marie A water bath or double boiler.

Bake To cook with dry heat, usually in an oven.

Bake Blind To bake a pastry shell without its filling.

Ballotine Boned, stuffed, and rolled meat or poultry that is served hot.

Baste To spoon or brush liquid over food while it is cooking.

Beard To remove the hairy appendages from mussels.

Beat To work a mixture until it is smooth.

Béarnaise A sauce of the Hollandaise family, which contains a reduction of vinegar, shallots, and tarragon.

Béchamel A rich white sauce.

Beurre Noisette Butter that has been heated until it turns light brown.

Bind To thicken a sauce with arrowroot, cream, or egg yolk.

Bisque A thick soup, usually made with shellfish.

Blanch To cook partially by submerging in boiling water.

Blend To mix two or more ingredients together thoroughly.

Boil To cook, submerged in water heated above 212° F.

Bouillabaisse A French fish soup.

Bouillon A broth made by cooking meat or fowl with vegetables.

Bouquet Garni An herb mixture consisting of a bay leaf, parsley sprig, thyme, and a celery stalk tied together in a cheesecloth bag.

Bouquetière A variety of vegetables arranged decoratively around food.

Braise To brown in a little fat and then simmer until tender in a small amount of liquid.

Bread To coat food with bread crumbs before cooking.

Brine   A pickling liquid usually containing salt and vinegar.

Brochette   A skewer usually used for broiling.

Broil   To cook directly under a flame.

Brown   To cook in a small amount of fat over high heat in order to seal in juices.

Bruise   To crush with either the side of a knife or the fingers.

Brunoise   To cut into fine dice.

Caramelize   To melt sugar until it becomes liquid and golden brown in color.

Cepes   Edible wild mushrooms, usually available dried.

Charlotte   A molded dessert.

Chill   To refrigerate until cold.

Chop   To cut food into small pieces.

Clarify   To remove impurities from a stock by adding egg whites and/or egg shells.

Coat   To cover food with flour or bread crumbs before cooking.

Coddle   To cook slowly in water that is just below the boiling point.

Consommé   Very strong clarified meat or poultry broth.

Cool   To lower the temperature of food by letting it stand off the heat.

Core   To remove the center of a fruit or vegetable.

Cornstarch   A thickening agent.

Coupe   An ice-cream dessert.

Court Bouillon   A fish broth used for poaching.

Cream   To beat shortening and sugar together until they are light and fluffy.

Crêpe   A thin pancake.

Crisp   To toast bread lightly in the oven; or to refresh salad greens in iced water.

Croutons   Small pieces of toasted or fried bread.

Cube   To cut into small squares of about one-half inch.

Cure   To preserve food using salt.

Cut In   To work shortening into a flour mixture until the mixture resembles coarse meal.

Decant   To gently pour wine from its original bottle into a server in order to remove any sediment in the original bottle.

Deglaze   To moisten a sauté pan with a liquid in order to dissolve the browned drippings in the pan.

Deep Fat   To cook food submerged in a boiling fat until the food is golden brown.

Dice   To cut into small cubes of less than one-half inch.

Dot   To cover the surface of food with small pieces of butter or cheese.

Dredge   To coat lightly, usually with flour.

Dust   To coat or sprinkle food with flour or sugar.

Duxelles   Minced sautéed mushrooms, usually used as a stuffing.

Farce   Stuffing or forcemeat.

Farci   Stuffed.

Fines Herbes   A mixture of chervil, chives, parsley, and tarragon.

Flake   To separate into small pieces.

Flambé   To pour liqueur over food and then to ignite it.

Florentine   Usually a dish made with spinach.

Flurries   Small pieces of butter.

Fold   To combine gently with a whisk or slotted spoon.

Forcemeat   A stuffing made of ground meat and seasonings.

French Fry   To cook food in deep fat.

Frizzle   To fry in fat until the edges of the food curl.

Frost   To cover with icing, whipped cream, or meringue.

Fry   To cook in a layer of hot fat.

Fumet   A concentrated fish broth.

Galantine   Boned, stuffed, and rolled meat or poultry that is served cold.

Garnish   To decorate.

Gherkins   Small pickled cucumbers.

Glaze   To cover with a thin shiny coating; to brown under direct heat.

Gratinée   To brown under the broiler.

Grease   To rub lightly with butter.

Grind   To put through a food chopper.

Hang   To age meat by hanging.

Ice   To chill food over ice; to cover a cake with frosting.

Julienne   To cut food into long thin matchlike strips.

Knead To work dough until it is smooth, elastic, and shiny.

Lard To insert strips of salt pork into meat using a larding needle;
  also a cooking fat.
Lardons Salt pork strips used for larding.
Liaison A binding agent of cream and egg yolks used for sauces and
  soups.

Macerate To steep food in liquid until it is softened.
Marinate To soak food in an acid mixture before cooking.
Marbling Grains of fat within the lean portion of a cut of meat.
Mask To cover completely.
Melt To heat a solid fat until it liquefies.
Mince To chop very fine.
Mirepoix A mixture of sautéed onion, carrots, and celery used as a
  flavoring agent.
Mix To stir until combined.
Moisten To add a little liquid.

Pan Broil To cook, uncovered, on top of the stove without fat.
Papillote Food cooked enclosed in foil or parchment paper to seal
  in the juices.
Parboiling To partially cook by boiling for a short period of time.
Pare To remove the skin.
Pâté A spiced ground meat mixture.
Paupiette A rolled, stuffed slice of meat, poultry, or fish.
Peel To strip off the skin; the skin or rind of a fruit.
Pickle To preserve in brine or vinegar.
Pinch The amount of a spice that can be held between the thumb
  and the first finger of the hand.
Pipe To decorate by forcing a dough, batter, icing, or whipped
  cream through the nozzle attached to a pastry bag.
Pit To remove the stones or seeds of fruit.
Plump To soak dried fruit in warm water or liqueur to soften it and
  to allow it to return to its original shape.
Poach To cook in water or broth that bubbles slightly; to simmer.
Pound To tenderize meat by hitting it with a meat mallet just until
  some of the cell structure is broken down. Do not try to double
  the size of the meat.

Preheat   To heat the oven to the temperature needed before using it.

Purée   Food pressed through a sieve, food mill, or ricer until it is pulpy; to liquefy in a food processor or blender.

Quenelles   Dumplings made of meat, poultry, or fish.

Ramekin   A shallow baking dish.

Reduce   To cook down over medium-high or high heat until there is only a small, concentrated amount.

Rice   To purée foods by forcing through a sieve or ricer.

Roux   Equal amounts of butter and flour cooked together to thicken a sauce.

Sauté   To cook quickly in a small amount of hot fat.

Scald   To heat liquid to just below the boiling point.

Score   To cut narrow gashes partway through the food.

Sear   To brown by intense heat.

Shred   To pull or cut meat or poultry flesh into very thin narrow slivers.

Sift   To shake through a sieve.

Simmer   To cook slowly at just below the boiling point.

Singe   To burn off the pinfeathers of plucked poultry.

Skim   To remove the scum or grease from the surface of a stock, soup, or sauce.

Sliver   Long narrow strips.

Steam   To cook on a rack over boiling water, without the water coming into actual contact with the food.

Steep   To soak in boiling liquid to extract an essence.

Stew   To cook in a liquid or sauce.

Stud   To insert a garnish, such as whole cloves, on the outside of food.

Suet   The protective fat around kidneys.

Sweetbreads   The thymus gland of a calf or lamb.

Tart   An open-faced pie usually made with custard and fruit.

Terrine   A container used to cook pâté.

Timbale   A small baking mold.

Toast   To brown the dry surface of foods.

Torte A rich cake whose batter is usually bound with ground nuts instead of flour.

Truss To tie up uncooked meat or poultry so that it will retain its shape after cooking.

Try Out To render the fat from poultry or meat skin.

Whip To beat rapidly until stiff and light.

Whisk To beat rapidly with a wire whisk.

Zest The colored part of the peel of citrus fruits.

Index